If **GOD** is
so good,
why do I
HURT
so bad?

If **GOD** is so good, why do I **HURT** so bad?

DAVID B. BIEBEL

Revell
Grand Rapids, Michigan

© 1989 by David B. Biebel

Published by Fleming H. Revell
a division of Baker Publishing Group
P.O. Box 6287, Grand Rapids, MI 49516-6287

New trade paperback edition published 2005

New Spire edition published 1995

Previously published in 1989 by NavPress

Second printing, November 2005

Printed in the United States of America

Library of Congress Cataloging-in-Publication Data
Biebel, David B.
    If God is so good, why do I hurt so bad? / David B. Biebel.
        p.   cm.
    Originally published: Colorado Springs, Colo. : NavPress, c 1989.
    Includes bibliographical references (p.   ).
    ISBN 0-8007-3108-5 (pbk.)
    1. Consolation. 2. Suffering—Religious aspects—Christianity.
3. Theodicy. I. Title.
BV4905.3.B52 2005
248.8'6—dc22   2005017614

This story is true, including its illustrations, excluding hypothetical cases, of course. Occasionally, certain facts or details have been altered to protect the privacy of individuals involved.

Unless otherwise noted, poetry is by the author.

Unless otherwise indicated, Scripture is taken from the HOLY BIBLE, NEW INTER-NATIONAL VERSION®. NIV®. Copyright © 1973, 1978, 1984 by International Bible Society. Used by permission of Zondervan. All rights reserved.

Scripture marked NASB is taken from the New American Standard Bible®, Copyright © 1960, 1962, 1963, 1968, 1971, 1972, 1973, 1975, 1977, 1995 by The Lockman Foundation. Used by permission.

To my parents, who laid the foundation for my faith in Christ, whose pain is mine as mine is his.

And to Christopher, a brave boy, whose pain became my path to learning, once again, that in my weakness he is strong.

Contents

Conclusions and New Directions

Acknowledgments

OTHER GUIDES HAVE written on the subject of suffering, and I would like to especially thank two of them, Peter Kreeft and Edward Kuhlman, for their encouragement and the thoughtfulness of their correspondence during this project. I have used some of their materials and incorporated some of their ideas throughout.

There are some other friends I'd like to thank for their input along the way, especially Truman Esau, M.D.; W. Glenn Jamison, M.D.; Alan Berggren, M.D.; Dale Matthews, M.D.; and my CMDS colleagues, Doug Knighton and Sid Macaulay. Speaking of CMDS and our general director, Hal Habecker, D.Min., I am grateful for the freedom allowed me to complete this book and the encouragement to do so, as well as access to the equipment and provision of the materials to support the task.

One of my best friends through this decade's musings and meanderings has been Helen Hosier, whom I cannot thank enough for her willingness to believe in me.

Also, I'd like to thank Karen Hinckley, this project's editor, whose helpful suggestions have sharpened my thinking and message. I have incorporated some of her ideas, and valued her critique, for "iron sharpens iron," and "faithful are the wounds of a friend."

And Ann, my wife, has been the best friend of all. Her faithfulness to me and her willingness to let me tell our story are continuing proofs of a love that I still can't comprehend.

Preface

ALL AROUND US, people are in pain. Emotional, physical, relational, spiritual—whatever its source, the pain feels the same.

Even born-again, sincere, evangelical, Bible-believing, church-going, church-leading believers are in pain. "There's a broken heart in every pew," said Joseph Parker, nineteenth-century British pastor. It's still true today.

Unfortunately, as someone else has noted, "The church is the only army that shoots its wounded," and the unrealistic expectations or even rejection that sometimes masquerade as spirituality can bring further injury instead of healing to people who desperately need it.

Many who hurt have been nursing the wounds for so long they can't remember what it's like to be anything other than sad. Others denied the pain and submerged the anger so long ago that they are unaware how the resulting depression, even bitterness, has subtly impacted their ability to love.

This book is for people in pain, especially from unresolved hurts, perhaps from years ago. By now you've exhausted everyone's patience and given up the hope that anyone understands or cares. You wish to have a heart-to-heart talk with somebody, but even when you pour out your feelings to God, you wonder if the words get past the ceiling.

If we could have some time together, I would do my best to listen to your story, and to share the things I've learned with you. But since we're limited now by distance, could I do the latter first?

Now I know it's possible you've heard a lot of principles and endured too much advice. So I'll skip most of that and try for something else: *truth*—one pilgrim to another. And the truth is, pain has *two faces*, human *and* divine. The human face is haggard, drawn, contorted, and streaked with tears. The divine is calm, assuring, kind, and loving—but likewise streaked with tears.

I've struggled with how to say what needs to be said, concerned that some may think that telling sounds profane, earthy, iconoclastic. But pain *is* profane, and isn't it time to stop cosmetizing it with pious platitudes as a mortician tries to hide the profanity of death?

This very day, not so long ago, certain women came with spices to cosmetize the crucified body of Jesus. How great their joy—and ours!—to find no cosmetizing necessary, for a most profane tragedy has been transformed by the power of God into the profoundest source of hope, the resurrection of our Lord.

If I could wish you anything, it would be that somehow, through the words that follow, you will find help and hope, but mostly that you will find him, the One who was broken that we might be made whole.

David B. Biebel
Easter Sunday 1989

1

Educated
at the
University

SALLY HAD BEEN a model patient as she fought her losing battle with lung cancer. She always had a smile for Dr. George, a medical resident whose visits with this fine Christian woman were like sunshine in his often dismal days. Two or three times a day, Sally would say how gracious the Lord had been to give her a Christian physician.

A nonsmoker herself, Sally's disease had probably been caused by exposure to her husband's four-pack-a-day habit. Initially her condition had improved, but now Dr. George had to deliver the unwelcome news that a very painful treatment she had undergone had failed, and she would have to endure it again.

"You have to have a second pleurodesis," he said. "The first one didn't take." They both knew his unspoken message was that nothing now was really going to help.

"You know, Dr. George," she said, "life's a struggle, and then you die."

The doctor's heart sank because he thought perhaps this trial had finally proven bigger than her faith, and he didn't know what to say. It wasn't until much later that he realized Sally's freedom to speak her feelings had come because she knew this doctor cared.

But long before he understood those dynamics, in fact by the very next day, his patient was once again her sunny self—radiant, in fact—despite her present and approaching pain.

For the doctor, it was one more lesson in his never-ending education at the University—a special school of higher learning called the University of Pain, a school that everyone attends sometime in life.

Pain is a school of higher learning because it is the place where earth and heaven meet and strive for mastery and meaning, reconciliation and peace. As Edward Kuhlman has said,

> "Pain" is the fundamental human predicament. No one escapes life without experiencing pain, although many become preoccupied with attempts to alleviate it. Pain is the overriding, inexplicable condition of life . . . the touchstone of our lives. In this "trysting place" heaven and earth meet. Here we meet each other in humanity, and more important, God meets us.[1]

But if pain is a place where we meet each other in humanity and even meet with God, why does speaking the truth about it sometimes sound like heresy, blasphemy, or worse? And why are hurting people sometimes asked, expected, or required to pretend about the way they really feel, when telling the truth is closer to godliness than pretending will ever be?

Whether it was illness, death, separation, divorce, infidelity, treachery, financial ruin, betrayal, or any other loss that brought your pain, somebody probably tried to "comfort" you with words like these: "All things work together for good." Or, "Keep your eyes on Jesus, and everything will be all right." And you nodded. What else could you do? They *were* telling the truth, after all.

But did they really want *you* to tell the truth—that is, if you could even put it into words?

It's doubtful.

Very few people are willing to listen, to truly hear your lament, to feel your anguish and share the pain, to cry with you until *you* have decided it's time to stop.

What happens for most hurting believers as a result is that they end up embracing only half the paradox of pain:

- Sometimes life is agony.
- Our loving God is in control.

Embrace only the first part, and you might as well write the epitaph of faith, "Died at thirty, Buried at seventy." Embrace only the second part, and your faith may survive, but I'll bet the farm that the rest of your pilgrimage will be marked by an inability to truly love God with your whole heart—the key to healing and wholeness. It's hard to sing, "Every day with Jesus is sweeter than the day before," when your heart of hearts is defiled by bitterness from anger at God you have never resolved.

There is another way, and that is what this book is about. God does not expect or require that we smile sweetly when he throws us in the mud. I loved this story from Peter Kreeft's wonderful book, *Making Sense Out of Suffering*:

> Even Teresa of Avila, when thrown off her carriage, slammed rudely to the ground, and deposited in a mud

puddle, questioned God. He answered her, "This is how I treat all my friends." Her tart reply was, "Then, Lord, it is not surprising that you have so few." Even saints do not smile sweetly when God throws them into mud puddles. Only pigs do that.[2]

That sweet, mud-covered smile you have been asked to wear is a mask you can put away for a while. It's not what God wants, because it's not real. And if it's not real, no matter how hard you try, it will ultimately prove ineffective in your effort to move beyond your pain or to help others with theirs.

"I've been longing to do that," you respond, with tears in your eyes to even *think* there's a way out. "But how do I know I can trust you?"

You can.

I'm asking you to take a risk. You have to take the chance that God is more loving, understanding, and forgiving than you have ever imagined. Because until you know he cares, you'll never really tell him how angry you are about what has happened.

And if you continue walking along with me, you'll be risking feeling some of those buried emotions all over again, and that can be almost as scary as feeling them for the first time.

I know.

I've been there. And I also know it's worth it.

And here's how I know.

Once upon a time, in a little town in Michigan's Upper Peninsula, there lived a young minister and his family. It was a nice little family. The pastor and his wife, Ann, loved each other very much. They were happy in their work and devoted to their children Jonathan and Allison—the light of their lives.

Jonathan, who was three years old, liked to go riding in the car with his daddy. One day as they rode along, the little boy posed an interesting question: "Daddy, if I was killed, would you still be able to find me?"

This daddy never answered. It was too painful for me to even think about the possibility that Jonathan had anything other than a wonderful, limitless future. He was beautiful, bright, and athletically gifted, the apple of my eye. I loved that boy—our first son—more than anything else in this world. It was impossible to think that anything other than happiness lay in store for us.

But the impossible happened. Late in the summer of 1978, Jonathan became ill with what seemed to be a normal childhood viral infection, with its accompanying symptoms. We expected he would recover in a few days, and we could get on with living. But he never did, and for us things changed forever.

Several mornings later, Ann called me at the office, "Davie," she cried, "will you come home and see if you can get Jonathan to talk right?"

I was home within seconds, since the church and parsonage were adjacent. But nothing I could do, or anything that anyone could do in the next five weeks, would change the fact that our beautiful, blond-haired, blue-eyed boy had suffered brain damage through some undiagnosed condition. He lingered awhile, but in early October, when the sugar maples are at their most glorious, he died.

The pain for we who remained was excruciating. Oh, I said the right words and did the right things, like speaking at both memorial services and repeating the words of Job as I committed his body to the ground on that New Hampshire hillside:

The LORD gave and the LORD has taken away.
Blessed be the name of the LORD.

Job 1:21 NASB

But when I buried Jonathan, I buried something of myself, because something had died in there, in my own heart of hearts. Was it faith? No, I clung to that, in spite of the anger, guilt, depression, doubts, and fears (which I documented in my first book, *Jonathan, You Left Too Soon*).

This poem is an excerpt from that part of my journey.

Lament

Destroy! Destroy! Our little boy,
What sad, demented mind, unkind
Would dare?
GOD?

Rebellion surges from my soul,
Unwhole, unwell, I, wounded,
Whimper.
WHY?

Reply! Reply! The silent sky,
The barren wasteland answers not
My cry.
ALONE?

Deserted? Or concealed? I wait
Relentless time to heal, reveal,
Explain,
THE PAIN.

The part of me that died was joy, at least the rather unfettered joy that Jonathan had brought to me. And one result, it took me almost eight years to realize, was a diminished ability to love God from the heart. Oh, I continued to serve him, obediently and energetically, and many were blessed during those years.

Preaching.
Teaching.
Counseling.
Surviving.

But I could not serve God with heart until I resolved the hurt. More on that later, because this story has another part.

That same country preacher returned home to New England in 1981, taking up a new ministry after welcoming a second son, Christopher, to the family in 1979.

I was glad for the change, but I was more glad to be away from the old than I was to be involved in the new—a symptom that took awhile to understand. The truth is, I was still depressed and in process. I knew that God's way leads toward joy, but it was hard to believe, sometimes, that I would ever again be anything but sad.

The healing came, slowly. But it came. And it came mostly through grappling with the issues in my doctoral work, writing a thesis report called, "Becoming a Whole Person," completed in 1986. Finally, this fragmented person was becoming whole again.

But I will never forget Friday, August 22, 1986, as long as I live. Because it was then, the second day of Christopher's illness, that it all came crashing back upon us, and we were thrown once again into the teeth of tribulation.

Brain damage—the doctors had confirmed it. Christopher was suffering from what was probably the very same extremely rare genetic disease that had killed Jonathan. They didn't even know for sure yet what it was.

After the doctors left the room, the pain rose up, broke me into little pieces, and then rolled over me. I sobbed like a baby, beyond comfort or control. "If that's the way it's going to be," I cried out from the depths of despair, "then God can go to . . ."

Is this what I get for serving God, even after our first loss? Isn't once enough?

But twice?

How can I serve a God like that?

How can I love a God like that?

These are the kinds of questions that might have echoed through my tormented mind if I'd been able to put them into words. Yet, that very night, as I neared my parents' home to tell them the awful facts, God took even my angry outburst and transformed it into a revelation of his redemptive love.

Suddenly, as I drove, I realized that God had *already* gone to hell, in the person of Jesus. And I knew that he had done so with a purpose, to redeem this sinful world—which allowed the possibility of genetic illness—and to redeem this sinful man, me.

Like a shaft of light into the darkness of my soul, that single insight lit the way toward peace. I could take you to almost the exact place in the road where God met me in my pain.

My words had been the cry of a broken heart, the outburst of a hurting child. God's words to me, as he held me close, might have been, "I understand, my son. I've been there already. I've felt your pain and carried your sorrows. I know your words arose from grief beyond control, and I love you still and always will."

Well, now *you* know how *I* know about pain.

And pain is pain. Perhaps its diversity is like the differences between Macintosh and Delicious apples, a continuum of hurting that makes your pain like mine and mine like yours.

The most hopeful thing, however, is not that your pain is mine and mine is yours, but that *ours is his*. And even more, that his healing can be ours.

But I'm getting ahead of myself.

Perhaps you are wondering what became of Christopher. I won't make you wait to find out, though I plan to weave the strands of that narrative together with others as we go. Just as I was composing the first draft of this first chapter, Christopher, Allison, and Dana (our second daughter) summoned their daddy downstairs to sample a creative concoction of water, dill, garlic, and baking soda they christened, "Pickle Fizz."

As we journey together, you'll hear about how Chris survived and has slowly recovered, though for awhile his future was in doubt. You will also hear how the rest of us have more than survived, as individuals and as a family, though there have likewise been moments of doubt about that.

And we want you to know from the outset, the reason we've survived is not because we're great (because the hurt has been bigger than we are). The reason we're intact today is that God is bigger yet than anything the evil one can send our way.

When **LOSSES** Come, They Can **BRING** . . .

2

Crisis

Learning My Limits

Was it David meets Goliath? Or Bambi meets Godzilla? For me, it was something like this: "Pastor, I have some bad news for you. Jonathan has died."

Though they were spoken in 1978, I can still hear those words today. I can picture the yard where we were. I can see the house. I can see myself, wandering to the side of the van, clenching my fists, fighting the tears.

"Why?"

And I can still feel the pain, though time has made it less intense.

How was it for you?

A phone call: "Hello, this is the police. . . . There's been a tragic accident."

A telegram: "We regret to inform you . . ."

A diagnosis: "Your son has . . . AIDS."

Conversations: "Did you hear about the pastor?"

25

Confrontations: "I don't think I love you anymore."
Words—scarcely heard and painfully recalled—invading your life, interrupting your plans, destroying your dreams, and etched forever in your memory.

Crisis.

It has many faces, all pocked by pain. Pain that often defies description. For crisis, by nature, is so intense that when you're in it, you can't express it, and when it's past, you can't remember the way it really was.

Perhaps the best and maybe the only way to describe crisis is through metaphor. Edward Kuhlman described how hearing the news of his sixteen-year-old son's disease overwhelmed him with a sense of fragmenting unreality:

> In that moment, my well-constructed world began to splinter into myriad pieces. Like a pane of glass shattered by a pebble, the fractures fanning out from the hole, I felt an overwhelming sense of unreality. . . . Like a canopy shrouding me in isolated disbelief, a sense of desolation and despair descended. I felt as if a flood had cascaded from a broken dam and swept me in its flow.[1]

For Peter Kreeft, learning of his five-year-old daughter's brain tumor (it was benign) was like a free fall into a lightless abyss:

> My stomach suddenly turned to mud and iron. . . . The truth could not be both known and felt at the same time. I had to split in half. If the truth had to be felt with the iron-and-mud gut, the same truth could not be accepted by the clear, thin light of the mind. For about two minutes I knew . . . the protective shell of withdrawal, a sanity-saving retreat from unbearable truth. This can't possibly be really happening to us. It's a bad dream. I can wake up in a minute, and it will all have gone away. The real world can't possibly be like that; it would be too absurd.[2]

26

For me in 1987, it was a journey to the limits, an instant trip to the edge of despair, like gazing into a deep canyon and wondering if I might as well jump:

> Crisis threatens to undo
> The glue of sanity. I cry
> Unwelcome tears, beyond control.
> And somewhere near the edge of soul
> I gaze into an empty hole,
> Abyss.
> Despair,
> With open arms awaits,
> And just beyond its diabolic gates,
> A bitter end,
> Futility.
> No pious platitudes suffice
> To penetrate the solid ice
> Of fear that grips my mind,
> As silent glacier slowly grinds
> Eternity to dust.
> And I, afraid that all is lost
> And nothing could redeem the cost
> Consider jumping, cast away . . .
> Or should I stay, for who can say
> That all is nothing,
> Nothing all?

In his anguish Job had cried, "What I feared has come upon me" (Job 3:25). Now I knew exactly what he meant. Like a *deja vu* nightmare, we were standing again by a hospital bed. Another place, another son, another grinding, searing pain beginning. As we waited, anxious and afraid, my eyes met Ann's, and without a word we both knew, the thing we'd greatly feared now had us in its massive jaws.

The crisis with Christopher developed slowly—little agonies mounting toward a cacophony of death. We fully expected to bury him. In my mind I did it many times. In fact, my imagination had me in that hole first. I remember looking out.

By Labor Day he began to perseverate, repeating words or sounds without being able to stop. Angry, I became gruff with him. "Stop it, Chris, stop it!" I grabbed him by the arms, looking him in the eyes, scaring him and showing me that dark side, the beast within—again. Reading the medical journal reports—the doctors suspected Leigh's disease, a degeneration of the central nervous system, which usually attacks children under two—left me in fear. Welcome back to the world of pediatric neurology!

The next night, before leaving for a second opinion in New York, I sat Chris on my lap, and prayed with him to receive Christ as his Savior. He couldn't speak for himself. "Do you love Jesus?" "Yup . . . yup . . . yup. . . ." Perseveration. Ten times, twenty times, you lose track. "Do you want him to come to live in your heart?" "Yup . . . yup . . . yup. . . ."

Chris cried. He knew what was happening, but not why. He was afraid. We were afraid. Was he slipping away? He laid back against my chest, looked up, and said, "I love you, Daddy."

We went to New York, returning with a faint glimmer of hope. Leigh's disease was ruled out. Another name, more rare—less than forty cases in the literature—took its place, Familial (usually called "Infantile") Bilateral Striatal Necrosis.

No prognosis.

For two months Ann and I watched our little son degenerate. Dying ourselves would have been much easier to bear. He had bilateral brain damage, and no one could tell us what we should expect.

On October 26, although he had seemed to be improving slowly, we couldn't rouse him for his late-night medication. Was it another attack, the beginning of the end? Would he ever wake again?

28

I climbed into bed with him, resolved that if another son of ours had to die, he wouldn't die alone. Before I fell asleep that night, with Chris cradled in my arms, I talked to him as he slept, "Daddy loves you. We all love you. Jesus loves you. You don't have to be afraid. If you don't wake up, you'll go to be with him . . . and we'll see you again . . . and we'll be happy, we'll be healthy, and we'll understand."

I will tell you more as we continue, but this is not so much my story, as *our* story—yours and mine. For now, I simply want you to know that I know about crisis.

But other people know about crisis too. And other languages sometimes give a broader view than ours. For instance, in Vietnamese the word for crisis is *Nguy-co* (Nwee-ker), literally, "danger-opportunity."

Crisis is both danger and opportunity. Let's think about it awhile, for even though crisis is inevitable in life, despair is not. Your emergence from this journey of pain as a wiser, stronger, more realistically faithful person will hinge almost entirely on how you look at things as you walk.

Crisis can take you to the limits. Looking both ways—toward despair *and* hope, doubt *and* faith—you may be hard pressed to choose, today. And the choice you make today will frequently change—tomorrow, if not before. It can be very confusing—more on that in the next chapter—but for now I would like to give you more than a "be happy" pill. Here is a little knowledge gained at the entry level of the University of Pain, Crisis 101:

- It will pass.

Now, before you throw this book away, remember, I know about crisis and I know about your pain. I would *never* make light of it, but I would like to *lighten* it.

29

Crisis is so consuming, it seems that it will *never* pass.

But it will.

Perhaps, looking back, you'll see the way the Lord has taught you things you otherwise might never have known. In a letter I wrote to Chris to celebrate his seventh birthday—about three months after he became ill—I expressed how learning my limits had taught me something about peace.

> Yet in the midst of it—awful and overwhelming as it really was—inside, way inside, I experienced a certain peace, or a calm that has made this time around so much different. Perhaps it is knowing that I have been to the very limit of my own soul's strength, come close to cursing God, and then discovered that I could not do it. My faith is real. It has true substance and it is secure—I am secure—because of a family relationship with the Almighty God who will not let me go even if I consider letting go of him. It was something I needed to learn, that I needed to know, and it's through your pain—our pain—that I've learned it. I know that no matter what happens I cannot go past the point where I was that night, and that is what gives me peace.

After Jonathan's death, I fought the pain. I never let it overwhelm me. What held me back was the fear that if I truly let myself go, I might never get back again to sanity.

The problem was, however, that in fighting it, I never really *felt* it. The second time I had no choice. It rose up, overwhelmed me, broke and crushed me before I had a chance to even look it in the eye. And—this may sound strange—I'm glad, because in that awful moment I learned what I could not have learned in any other way: my limits. Even beyond that terrifying brink of sanity, there was something (actually, someone) holding me up, and holding me together as my whole world was falling apart.

It was a dangerous place to be, but a singular opportunity . . .

To know that in my weakness, he is strong.
To learn to trust, even when I cannot feel the ground.
To understand that I am no master of my destiny.
To become wiser and more real.

There is yet another danger: in your anger, frustration, resentment, bitterness, and pain, you may begin to fear that hope of being reconciled with God is lost forever.

It's not.

Your capacity for pain is an indicator of your capacity for joy. Your friends may never understand, but take it from one who does. Your ability to feel is as important as your ability to think. Both are part of your eternal self, a reflection of the image of God in you.

He made you that way, with a beauty and variety that for now may threaten to undo you, may seem more curse than blessing, a risky, dangerous place to be.

It is.

Peter Kreeft, in a letter to me, explained it this way:

Capacity for pain and joy, hate and love, sin and sanctity, are together. God loves capacity, potentiality, risk: that's why he created us with free will. What terrifyingly wild, risky, apparently-irresponsible desires he must have! Job's whirlwind, not our safe, nice, conceptual pyramid. Aslan is not a tame lion.

Your friends may preach their "pyramids" of faith, pious platitudes, and pharisaic principles to cage the lion and calm the whirlwind, when God is going somewhere else with you.

Take God's hand. He knows how you groan inwardly (see Rom. 8:23), and he understands and cares. He's been there for you, and he is with you now, interceding for you with "groans that words cannot express" (Rom. 8:26). In your coming passage, that may lead through confusion and fragmentation toward peace, you can have no better friend.

For, unlike your other friends, God cannot let you walk alone.

3

Confusion

What's Wrong with Me?

I SUPPOSE YOU thought that knowing God would make your struggle easier. Somebody told you so. Maybe *everyone* told you so. Why then has it been so hard to move beyond your pain?

One of the best kept secrets about processing pain from the perspective of faith is this: your relationship with God can make it *harder* before it makes it easier. The good news is that the faith-walk remains the only way to transform this pain into anything other than pain.

Without faith, I'm left alone with fate. By some unfortunate twist of fate—impersonal, dispassionate, enigmatic chance—my dreams lie shattered on the ground. For a while, perhaps a long while, I may rage, protest, do everything in my power to register my complaint, but the time finally arrives when I realize that continuing to beat my head on this brick wall is pure futility. I might as well accept it and get on with living, since there's nothing I can do to change what's happened. I'll just have to make the best of it, somehow.

If I have a faith-relationship with God, however, the dynamics are radically different. My rage is more focused and my indignation personal, since both he and I are persons. My struggle to understand no longer self-destructs against an impenetrable wall. My protests do not echo through a mindless chasm. Does this pain have any meaning? Does this pilgrimage have a purpose?

Faith makes the process personal. And although this does hold promise for resolution as opposed to resignation, for a while things can become quite bewildering.

The pain may intensify. Beyond the loss that brought me here is the pain of knowing it is from the Father's hand. He may not have *caused* it, true, but he certainly must have allowed it. He could have intervened. Why did it have to happen this way? Why did it have to happen to us?

The confusion may compound. How can *this* be love? And how can I love him, if this is what I get for it? Not only must I be reconciled with some unacceptable event, but I must also be reconciled with the one I hold responsible.

Then add the fear that these intense feelings and endless questions may further jeopardize our relationship. If God grows weary of my whining, annoyed with my complaints, might not the fire fall again? The guilt and doubt and anger and pain go round and round, rendering a normally rational person temporarily impaired.

Marian's daughter was killed in a fiery car crash, and she was left to wander on, confused. In a personal letter, she expressed her thoughts:

> I didn't pray the morning she was killed or the eve before. This causes me pain and guilt. There are other things—I, too, have gone over and over my sins. . . .
>
> I question, where is my deep faith? Why do I have these doubts about her safety [in God's presence]? I think God must be very impatient with me.

34

I'm so limited. I think I really have a hard time believing that God cares enough for me to know the number of hairs on my head. I'm at fault for diminishing His Greatness into human confines. . . . The masses of people and the vastness of the sky scare me so.

I try to relinquish her to God each morning for that day. I feel I'm in constant prayer. Why don't I feel God's direction and nearness?

. . . I'm so inadequate now. I can only survive this world by serving God and by loving and serving others. Oh, please answer me—what's wrong with me . . .

Losses can bring intense confusion. This is true even for . . .

Bible-believing,
God-fearing,
Sincere,
Born-again,
Church-going,
Evangelical
Christians.

Somebody probably tried to hand you a spiritual "be happy" pill as an answer to your pain, implying that what you're experiencing is a "spiritual problem." If only you would pray more, confess your sins, repent, go to church, read the Word, practice the pastor's five steps for overcoming depression, *ad nauseam*.

Simple answers will not suffice. This confusion involves the whole person—soul, body, and spirit.

- Thoughts conflict: belief, doubt, hope, despair.
- Feelings collide: anger, guilt, fear, low self-esteem.
- Choices vary: submission, rebellion, lethargy.

- Health suffers: restlessness, tension, anxiety symptoms.
- Spirit groans.

And you wonder, will I ever be normal again?
What's wrong with me?
I wrote back to Marian, "NOTHING is wrong with you! You are passing through the valley of the shadow of death. You are experiencing an extreme grief reaction because of the nature of your loss, and I can assure you there is nothing WRONG with you as far as I am concerned."

This kind of confusion is *normal* for people struggling with loss, *especially* believers. Remember, others can just walk away, their protests dissipating into an apparently heartless universe.

But you—you believe that God loves you, and that in everything he causes or allows he is motivated by that love, and that as your heavenly Father, he has in mind only what will ultimately be for your best. Reconciling these paradoxical ideas may take some time, perhaps a long, long time.

What if they never come together? What if you struggle and wrestle and grapple, earnestly striving to understand, only to reach the ultimate conclusion that you cannot make perfect sense of it?

Well, then, you are in good company. I don't mean just company with me. The "Saints Hall of Fame"—Hebrews 11—is crowded with people who did not fully understand, but they *did* keep walking by faith despite the ambiguities. And who can explain what Jesus meant when, hanging on the cross, he cried out in agony, "My God, my God, why . . . ?" (Matt. 27:45).

Sometimes we simply cannot know why. God's ways are not our ways, nor are his thoughts ours (see Isaiah 55). If you have been searching for answers, especially if your wilderness wandering has been extended, you've probably heard enough inane opinions and foolish speculations to last a lifetime.

How often others rush to offer reasons—as if God needs a mouthpiece. "If only you'd done this, or if only you hadn't done that." My father—also a minister—received an almost laughable indictment when Christopher was stricken. The letter laid the blame for God's apparent judgment on our house at my father's feet for his failure to use only the King James Version of the Bible in his preaching.

Father, forgive that intruder. He didn't know what he was saying, playing God for us when what he really needs is to know you as you really are.

I think "Job's comforters" offer their empty words of judgment and advice not so much to help us as to extricate themselves from a major difficulty: their system doesn't work. Oh, it works okay in the good times. "Good things happen to godly people!" And "godly people" is defined by a vast web of intricate pharisaical rules.

But when trouble finds your tent—you, who were formerly one of us—the system threatens self-destruction, unless someone intervenes. Enter Job's comforters, defenders of the faith, interpreters of truth, self-appointed spokesmen for God.

Can you pray that God will forget their foolishness and disregard their drivel? And can you pray that God will protect you from believing a lie, embracing answers to their inquisition when the things he wants to teach you are beyond their system's reach?

When you're in pain, the problem is that it is *much* easier to surrender to the accusers than to resist their assault. For one thing, you don't have the energy to resist. For another, you, like them, long for resolution. Answers, even self-condemning ones, seem better than no answers at all. Even guilt seems better than the anxiety of not knowing.

Ann turned to me one night and said, "This time, God is punishing me." I tried to tell her the blame for this had nothing to do with us, personally—the potentiality for genetic deficiency came into our universe with the fall. And if she is God's target, the rest of us less godly sinners better take cover.

Sometimes pain brings such confusion. She struggled for months to move beyond the guilt, false as it was. The "accuser" (Rev. 12:10) dragged her to the judgment. She was a convict in the courtroom of her own mind.

But we have an advocate with the Father, Jesus Christ the righteous One (see 1 John 2:1–2), who loved us enough to pay the penalty for *all* our sins at Calvary—long before we were even thought of, in purely human terms—because we were in his mind, even then. And he continues to love us now and to intercede for us (see Rom. 8:34), perhaps as he prayed for Peter, "Simon, Simon, Satan has asked to sift you [the Greek plural seems to refer to the whole group] as wheat. But I have prayed for you, Simon, that your faith may not fail. And when you have turned back, strengthen your brothers" (Luke 22:31–32).

God has his own timetable and reasons for things. He didn't *have* to grant Satan's request to sift the disciples. He didn't *have* to allow the affliction of Job (see Job 1:1–2:11). He didn't *have* to allow your path to pass through the valley of pain.

God doesn't even have to reveal his reasons for things, and my conviction is that if he ever does so, it is very unusual. But we can know the larger truths. We can see the bigger picture of how he accomplishes his redemptive work in the world, even how he wants to do so through our pain. But as to "Why this?" "Why now?" and "What did I do to deserve this?" it may be awhile.

The simple truth about your pain is that you may never understand the "Whys" this side of glory. A deeper truth is that God can redeem your pain into power, anyway. Perhaps even more profound may be the conclusion that

38

your faith will be stronger if you *can't* understand than it will be if you *do*. In other words, while we struggle to make it clear, or travel the world to find someone who can, it may be the father's plan, instead, that we learn to live with ambiguity.

In a letter to Edward Kuhlman, I admitted,

> "Answers" have not come easily for me, either. More questions than answers, sometimes. The ambiguity confounds and inspires simultaneously. But I've been thinking about my rather free, but accurate, translation of 1 Corinthians 13:12, ". . . for now, we understand . . . as in a riddle. . . ." The reflection/riddle is the best we can do, for now, in our quest to know ultimate truth. I find it interesting that Paul's introduction to chapters 12–14 . . . begins, "Now concerning spiritual [matters]" (12:1 NASB). I really think, considering the Corinthians context, that he meant "spiritual persons." If so, it is a mark of spirituality to know that I don't know, that the mystery of life becomes known to me now ONLY as a riddle.
>
> Beyond that, perhaps it is BEST known as a riddle. . . . For a riddle loses its mystery, power, even its significance, once it is solved. Perhaps by keeping us in the riddle, unable to extricate ourselves by solving it, God has protected us from apathy and indifference. Or perhaps it is protection from the unbearable (undoubtedly fatal) burden that knowing what he knows would [be for] . . . our deficient minds.

To solve God's riddle is to destroy it. Much of his wisdom is learned through metaphor and parable. Modern Christians sometimes rush to put his truth into little boxes, neatly systematized, categorized, organized, and principalized, when God's perspective on suffering is too big for any of that. While for some, "spirituality" is defined by what you know, for God it may be more how you handle what you *cannot* know.

The human mind seeks solutions, so we pose the "problem of pain." Perhaps, instead, we should be searching for clues. As Peter Kreeft wrote,

> The true answer [to the question of suffering] might be so mysterious and deep that we couldn't get it all at once. It might be like a story. (Tell me the whole story of David Copperfield all at once, or at least in twenty-five words or less, please.) It might be like a person. Reduce a person to a category, to a stereotype. It can't be done. If the answer is like a story or like a person, that would be a richness, not a defect. We would then be glad it is a mystery rather than a problem.[1]

I'm not saying that *everything* is ambiguous, as do certain theologies that seem to make selective ignorance a matter of sophistication. God has made everything we need to know for life (present and eternal) and godliness clear enough that even a child can understand it. But in the context of suffering, we may be learning this truth: to embrace an abiding ambiguity is the essence of trust. Sometimes we simply *cannot* understand, but is it enough to know who does? Link yourself to God by faith. Listen with your inner ear as he keeps softly saying, "I love you." Believe that he can guide you through this wasteland to a better place. Ask your questions, all of them, because the asking itself is an affirmation that you know a person and you live in relationship. And that fact, beyond your attempts to loose yourself from this riddle called life, is what will carry you beyond the confusion you may experience today.

Do you think God cares? Here is the way our daughter Allison expressed her thoughts as she grappled at age nine with another brother's illness and how the complete focus of her parents' energies on Christopher meant, for her, another year of going without much attention. She

would lie in bed, looking out the large picture window
at the stars, and cry.

Life Eyes

As life goes by some things change
    but others seem just to stay.
I've always known that He is with me
    but now I know He sees right through me.

I feel as though I've been cheated
    one whole year, and no chance to complete it.
Some people say that life is fair
    though from my experience I feel as though
        God doesn't care.

I used to wonder if my life would break,
    when the next sob I would take.
When I lie alone in bed,
    the place for where I rest my head.
I see the stars and moon above
    and that is when I know I'm loved.

4

Fragmentation

When Life's No Fairy Tale

"I CAN'T TAKE it anymore!" Ann cried, as she stumbled toward me. For more than a month she had been with Chris every possible moment. She would have stayed with him around the clock if she'd had the strength. Tenaciously, she fought the increasing tone in his arms and legs. Slowly, the brain damage was forcing his body into a tight little ball. Courageously, faithfully, she straightened his legs, his feet, his arms, his fingers—ten times, fifty times, a hundred times a day. When he was awake and when he was asleep, she gently hovered over Chris, unwilling to let the process have him.

But she had passed her limits. Exhausted and broken, she was about to go under in our turbulent storm. She had to have help, which we arranged as quickly as we could. But even that left her with guilt, because she had

43

somehow failed to handle what everyone else could see was an overwhelming situation.

Only a week earlier, I had written in the journal how fortunate Christopher was to have Ann for a mother: "Only a handful of women . . . could handle this—you have one of them." A statement I still affirm, and always will.

But every person has limits, even

Bible-believing,
God-fearing,
Sincere,
Born-again,
Church-going,
Evangelical
Christians.

And every relationship has limits. Even Christian marriages, friendships, and other relationships sometimes break when hammered by severe stress. No amount of pretending will change that fact. So in this chapter, while writing about us, I've chosen to also write about you, your marriage, your family, your friends, your relationships. For you are part of a system of relationships, and the whole system is impacted by your pilgrimage through the valley of pain.

When your crisis came, time stopped for you. But it also stopped for your spouse, your children, the larger family, your friends, and possibly even your community. All of them wondered, and prayed, and hoped, and cried, waiting for news, good news.

Perhaps no good news ever came, no light, only darkness. Days became weeks. The pain became unbearable, and you withdrew into yourself—the only safe place—to grapple with this thing in privacy. And the more you struggled, the more it seemed the others moved away, leaving only you to rage, rage against an inexpressible injustice.

As you wandered through this wilderness, your friends and family became like strangers, and if you're married, your marriage almost became a statistic.

Our marriage almost became a statistic. And since I want you to know how I know about your personal and relational fragmentation, I'm going to risk revealing some very personal facts about us.

On two occasions Ann and I discussed going separate ways, which would have been a physical expression of what was happening on other levels. I distinctly recall how things seemed to reach a climax for both of us about three months into Christopher's illness.

During the day I had slapped Christopher—three times—for continuing to make a grunting or snoring sound after I asked him to stop. Somehow that mindless noise tapped my fears of his future as a potentially handicapped person, and I was briefly beyond control.

That night, we talked over our need for help. However, because of my pride, I failed to focus on my mounting desperation, confronting Ann's depression instead, exhorting her to choose. Happiness comes from within, I reminded her, it's an inner thing. And she was so sad.

But I, too, was sad, realizing that I was now on the periphery of her life, and I didn't like it. She was so absorbed in what was happening to Chris, and I longed for intimacy, almost begging, "Don't shut me out. Don't shut me off."

One of the battlefields in this unfortunate, but common, conflict was our bedroom. We had always enjoyed a mutually fulfilling sexual relationship—except when Jonathan had been sick—and now we had problems again.

I needed a release from the incredible tensions, and she was feeling empty, dead, inside. How could she experience pleasure, allow herself a little joy, when only a few feet away in his own room lay little, suffering Christopher?

Emotionally speaking, she was drained, flat, a shell of herself. In addition, she was feeling guilty for past things and associating the fact that our sons had been stricken with genetic illnesses with the act that had brought them into being. For her, the resolution of this particular factor became a difficult and lengthy passage, guided by a Christian counselor.

I tried to provide what she needed in the bedroom—nonsexual intimacy, somebody to hold her—without becoming too demanding. Looking back, I appreciate her willingness to fulfill my needs, even when she had no inclination to do so. Those weren't among my most satisfying times, either, for sex is so much more fulfilling when it is both giving and receiving. But, speaking candidly, it was her willingness to meet my needs, even if I wasn't meeting hers, that was a major factor in keeping us together.

Another thing that helped greatly was that, just as we were dealing with our sexual conflict, someone offered an opportunity for us to get away for a few days. It was the best thing that could have happened, though I did some manipulating and cajoling to convince Ann that the kids would be okay for a couple of days without us. "Trust me," I wrote in the journal. "You've been absorbed into a blob with only your eyes sticking out."

Fortunately, she did trust me, and things worked out marvelously. We had some time with the kids at a resort, where Chris was able to kick his legs in the pool—giving us hope for his recovery. Then we had some time by ourselves—to talk, listen, reflect, relax, and renew our relationship on many levels.

But complex needs are not resolved overnight, nor is there any easy fix for the interpersonal fragmentation that intense losses can bring. We returned to the same house, to the same unspeakable private hell, *and* to the same bedroom. It really took at least another six months to rebuild our relationship.

During that time—I say this with deep regret—I turned to another person for support. She was a bright, young, vivacious, professional woman I'd met on one of my trips. When we had a chance to talk, she would listen to me and sympathize with me. She was interested in my thoughts and appreciative of my talents, at a time when Ann just didn't have any reserves for my secondary needs.

I felt young again, and alive in ways I only dimly recalled from adolescence. I began to find in this other person—when I allowed my imagination to wander—a different incentive to leave the negatives I encountered each time I walked in our door. If it had gone much further, I might have even embraced the lie that (considering the rather abject pain I had faced) nothing really mattered, ultimately, including my own personal morality.

Another kind of fragmentation was beginning: the division between the new self that wanted to serve God and love Ann in faithfulness and truth, and the old self that, at the moment, was considering throwing all the rest away for a momentary and passing pleasure.

The good news is this: the old self lost—but not without an energetic struggle lasting several months. It was Romans 7 on the battlefield of my soul, another opportunity to learn that no one is exempt, anyone can fall, anyone.

I came to my senses just in time. Sitting at my computer, I was writing to a friend, and I had just written that I was experiencing a serious personal temptation and wouldn't he please pray for me, when I realized that I didn't need to write about this to anyone. I needed to deal with it before the sin that was crouching at my door moved beyond what had been a dangerous flirtation with disaster to devour everything I had lived and taught.

So I called the other woman. I thanked her for the positive things she had given me and the lessons I had learned, but explained that I could not give myself to her because I had given my heart to Ann.

And then I told Ann, which I don't necessarily recommend if you're experiencing similar issues, since it can seem to place the blame for our unfaithfulness on our mate when he or she may already be carrying an unbearable load. I suggest instead that you find a respected marriage counselor and seek, with godly guidance, to understand the forces and needs within yourself that are about to destroy your marriage.

When I stripped everything else away, the thing that kept me faithful—not perfect, but I never promised that—was my commitments. In 1969, I had made a commitment to Ann to keep myself for her, as long as we both should live, and although I had managed to come close to violating that covenant, I was still hers if she wanted me.

In 1974, I had entered the ministry, trying to teach by word and example what faith in God can mean. When that commitment had been tested in 1978 with Jonathan's death, I had repeated the commitment at a conference of my peers: "I would rather be a doorkeeper in the house of my God than dwell in the tents of the wicked" (Ps. 84:10).

I had many commitments to fulfill: to God, to Ann, to our children, to our larger family, to all the people I had led and taught, as well as to our friends—and even to the other woman, through confession and forgiveness for such foolishness. And the reason I mention all of these commitments—in fact, the reason I have taken the risk of telling about these dynamics at all—is that I know you may be struggling with similar issues.

I want you to win! Don't give in. Keep the faith.

In order to do that, you need to know that no starry-eyed adolescent love will sustain you in this kind of testing. Only solid commitments, based on covenants with God, yourself, and the people in your life, will give you the power to turn away from this trap of the evil one, preserving the possibility of someday building a deeper relationship with your spouse than you've ever had before.

But what if you have failed already, and fallen? Even then there can be forgiveness, reconciliation, a restoration that can lead to a deeper love relationship with your mate. With God, there is always hope. But introduce adultery into an already impaired relationship and the dynamics become even more intense, along with the need for professional assistance. For you *and* your mate may already be exhausted emotionally, physically, spiritually—in every way, almost bankrupt. And the added stress of infidelity may so magnify the negatives that the only option seems to be divorce.

It's not. But the work you'll have to do now is even greater than what stared you in the face before. I hope you'll choose to do it, nonetheless. Because any other route toward resolution is a lie. Take your pain to someone else—or something else—and you may be shocked how it can rapidly compound instead of diminishing.

Trust me. I know something about even that. But since I've already revealed enough true confessions illustrating my weaknesses, I don't feel compelled to tell you many more. So I won't tell you how long it took me to cement those commitments, or how much pain Ann endured as she tried to relate to me during that time. Neither will I tell you the part that alcohol—a common means of trying to escape—played in the whole scenario.

But I will tell you that as a result of this ugly chapter in our marriage, I came to understand how so many people choose to separate and walk away from each other, in a vain effort to escape the pain. And I will also tell you I am glad beyond words that we didn't.

Why would I tell these things at all? Because I believe *most* people experiencing severe stress begin to seek inappropriate means of escaping the pain. And many, if not most, who are married will at least consider going separate ways, for one reason or another, but mostly because they have never faced the fact that since their loss they have been gradually drifting apart. By the time that realization sinks in, they have already diverged so far that it seems easier to turn away and start over with someone else than to turn back and try to rebuild what has been disintegrating.

Most people assume that a common loss drives the people involved together, and that their mutual pain then cements their relationship with an everlasting bond. Let's let the secret out. In reality, pain is a better wedge than it is a glue. Because regardless of its intensity, the people in the "family system" experience the same loss individually, often choosing divergent paths in their quest for peace.

No one, not even your closest companions, will ever know exactly how you hurt. Your pain is uniquely yours. And their pain is uniquely theirs even though you may not be quite ready to think about that yet because you're mostly focused on your own pain.

Expecting compassion and understanding from those closest to you, you find instead that each is caught up in his or her own process, battered or even broken by the struggle. Perhaps they were even hoping to receive support from *you* when you feel you have nothing more to give. It's a double-bind, lose-lose situation.

Is there any hope?

Yes.

First, *get help! Don't try to fix it yourself.*

It's too risky, and the stakes are too high. Find someone to walk with you through this fragmenting time, a nonjudgmental, loving Christian friend or counselor who will listen and help you sort things out before it all comes apart.

Sadly, you may not find what you need in the church. So, if that is true, thank the Lord for the good things your church does provide, and find your compassionate listeners elsewhere. Usually there are groups established and functioning where you will find others, like yourself, who are trying to put the pieces of their own lives back together somehow.

Second, *consider your larger family system.*

A whole book needs to be written on this subject from a Christian perspective, because it is a proven fact that significant loss impacts *everyone* in the family system, and even beyond. Life stops for them when it stops for you.

Consider your children, for instance, if your husband has died or deserted you. For you it may seem that yours is the primary loss, but what about them? They have lost a father, but they have also lost the part of you and the part of each that they could know only through him. Do you know how they feel, and how much they are now forced to relate to you and to each other differently?

Or perhaps one of the children is injured or sick. How are the others relating to that event and to all the other players on the stage? Allison wrote to her school counselor:

Dear Mrs. C.,
   I'm mad! I'm upset. I'm sad. I hate myself, I hate being fat, I'm discouraged and uncertain. I feel mixed up and very weird. I want to be mad at somebody.
   . . . I just want to let it all out and cry. I want to just go somewhere with somebody and scream. I feel really depressed about all this stuff that's going on. I am mad at my mom. I'm mad at my dad, and myself for not being able to help [Chris] these past few days. I have really been praying that God will help him get better, but nothing has happened so now I'm mad at God, too.
   Love,
   Allison
P.S. Please write back.

Members of your extended family may sometimes wonder how they can share your pain—for it is their pain too. Can you let them into it, instead of being so possessive?

I recall how hard it was for my brother Dan to reach me when Chris was hospitalized in New York. Dan, like everybody else, was anxious to know what was happening. Strangely, neither Dan nor I can remember now whether or not I called him back. My conscience tells me I didn't, but either way, I certainly could have made it easier for him. But telling the tale of woe again, even to family—or perhaps *especially* to family—was like twisting the knife in the wound. Sometimes it was all we could do to manage the pain we already carried. But I owed it to him. My tears were his, and his pain was mine.

What about your friends? They really don't know what to say, because there isn't anything that *can* be said that would help much, except, "I love you." And sometimes they're not even sure you want to hear that. How can they help when it seems that all you want to do is focus on your loss? Most people don't want to dwell on what was, or might have been, because then they won't be able to experience what is.

Third, try to *let yourself believe there will be life again,* someday—perhaps even life you can enjoy. As Ann was sliding away into the muck of despair, I tried to give her hope, "There will be life after this," I offered.

"Oh, no, there won't," she replied.

There is.

For all of us.

And there can be for you!

5

Putting the Pieces
Back Together

- Isn't it time to get on with living?
- Isn't it over yet?
- How long are you going to live in the past?
- If you wanted to you could be such a comfort to others.
- If you'd only open your eyes you would see that many people have it worse than you.
- If your faith was stronger, you wouldn't be having such a struggle.

Depending on how long you've been suffering, somebody has said one or all of these things to you. You probably responded with a sigh, a nod of resignation, angry resentment, or true agreement. After all, if you are a child of God, you know that his desire is your wholeness, even your joy. Do you dare to believe it? Can you even imagine a deep and abiding inner peace?

In fact, if Jesus were to speak to you right now, he might gently look into your eyes and ask, "Do you want to get well?" as he did of an invalid by the pool of Bethesda (see John 5:6)—a strange request, really, since the man had been lame for thirty-eight years. Close your eyes for a moment and imagine Jesus before you, looking toward you, speaking those words to *you*: "Do you want to get well?"

How long have you been lame? That is really what happens to us when we wrestle with God. Jacob did it, emerging from the encounter lame but with a new name, "Israel," meaning, "he struggles with God" (see Gen. 32:22–30). As Edward Kuhlman wrote, in the process,

> the independent, self-reliant Jacob learned the lesson [of dependency] . . . and forever after he limped along, halting upon his thigh. He had a visible dependency upon God. . . . The staff upon which Jacob leaned (Heb. 11:21) was the crutch that became his identification mark. From a swagger stick of arrogance to a support of humility—the long lesson of dependency.[1]

Notice:

It's okay to wrestle with God.
Jacob did it.
Job did it.

But don't expect your Christian friends to understand what's going on. In fact, like Job's friends, they may criticize, judge, and reject you if you express what's really on your mind.

Try to forgive them. They don't understand that most believers go through at least three stages in grappling with significant loss. Perhaps you didn't expect it yourself.

At first, you affirmed your faith.

I remember standing on that New Hampshire hillside on that beautiful October day in 1978, repeating the words of Job as we committed Jonathan's body to the ground.

Orthodoxy.
Obedience.
Faithfulness.
Affirmation.
Numbness.

I cannot feel anything. Like a puppet dancing on some celestial string, I speak what I know, forcing myself to do what I have to do—or what I should do.

But deep inside the storm begins, gathering force as it feeds on uncried tears and broken dreams. It overwhelms my faith and drives my heart before it, like a rowboat in a hurricane.

Grief's second phase involves tremendous conflict, as emotions dominate the mind, struggling to express what cannot easily be put into words: frustration, anger, resentment, rage, guilt, remorse, anxiety, confusion, fear, despair.

Perhaps the greatest fear is that what has happened has no meaning—that, indeed, the opening words of Ecclesiastes are the only truthful obituary: "'Meaningless! Meaningless!' says the Teacher. 'Utterly meaningless! Everything is meaningless'" (Eccles. 1:2). This fear sometimes drives people to try to redeem value from an otherwise seemingly senseless tragedy. Some write books. Others build memorials or establish scholarships. Some devote their remaining years to social or political action groups, especially groups that address the situation that caused their loss.

These constructive activities can be very worthwhile, and in a certain sense they are even redemptive. But we cannot create meaning. We can only discover it. If a loved one has left us, his life *had meaning*, whether or not we can see it now, and whether or not it lasted as long as we think it should have. We don't have to *do* anything to create what already exists, although we may work hard to preserve it.

Perhaps we can see this value best when we think about death before birth, as in miscarriage. People's lives have *intrinsic* meaning—not because of their achievements or their quality of life or their usefulness to society, but because they were made by God in *his own image*. This meaning is not ours to create, but his.

While you're in grief's middle stage, it may be difficult, perhaps impossible, to focus your faith that clearly. Sometimes it's hard enough just to think clearly at all. In fact, the conflict between mind and emotions, faith and doubt, may become so intense that things like hope and despair somehow seem alike. But, then again, perhaps they *are* similar. And it's only in the topsy-turvy times when our categories are being challenged, even expanded, that the broader dimensions of certain truths can be known at all.

My journal suggested that hope and despair seemed alike somehow. Through his correspondence, Peter Kreeft helped me understand:

> Hope and despair are alike (1) in that both are total, all-embracing, not able to specify and define their object. Jonathan was for you a symbol of life itself. Without ceasing to be Jonathan, he sacramentally represented, or re-presented, the whole. Only a person can do that. Thus his death invited you to despair not just of him but of life. Hope, likewise, was not only for the recovery of the part

but the whole. Jonathan was both: part of the whole and a whole. Every person is, but we perceive the fact that a person is more than a part, an ingredient, only by love.

Hope and despair are also alike (2) in that they face an ultimate choice. No Laodicean lukewarmness, no indifference remains open as a third option. It is either/or.

Third, they *feel* the same. Both hit you in the gut, not the head. The greatest sweets are bitter-sweets. The greatest beauty is always watered by tears. That is a fact, the explanation is beyond me, except that both involve ecstasy, self-transcendence, self-forgetfulness, standing in something unhandleably enormous.

Back and forth I went. Sometimes hoping, sometimes despairing—my heart the pendulum, the fixed point my faith. Only later could I write this conclusion to Edward Kuhlman:

> We live by the promises—we die by their falsehood. . . . Crises force us to evaluate the truth of the promises. . . . Is this a lie? Is it all meaningless? Without faith, hope is humanistic and vain before the ultimate crushing blow of death. Without God, hope *is* despair, because it is without substance . . . a vain self-deception.

Faith is the thing that got me through the middle phase again. Faith that even though life can be a bitter disappointment, our living God is in control. But there was tremendous inner tension and frustration, sometimes expressed in dreams, sometimes in violence (as when I punched through a wall after six hours of hearing Chris's whimpering from the pain and seeing his almost constant spasms and dystonia).

Sometimes my faith was weak, as when I wrote in the journal:

> I'm about to chuck my faith. If there is a God and if he could do anything about it, why doesn't he? There are

many faithful men and women all over the country praying and claiming [Chris's] healing. Keep the faith. I'll try, but, God, it's so hard to watch the slow destruction of our second son.

It was so hard to hope. "Do I believe—dare to believe," I wrote, "hope that he will get better? The joy would be almost as painful as the pain so far."
Sometimes it was just hard to exist, as when, following a weekly visit with the neurologist, I wrote in the journal:

Severe depression . . . almost suicidal—afternoon reached conclusion that I would/could not continue in the ministry. Went to talk with Dad regarding the implications of that [we shared pastoral duties in a small fellowship]. . . . He was outside in the cold and wind, so I came home instead . . . ate and took a rest. In the beginning, I wanted to die . . . take me away from this. I don't think I can forgive God for this if Chris stays the same. End of nap, I woke thinking of my own counseling.

Reflecting on the events of the past couple of days, I could see how I had become so physically and emotionally, even spiritually, exhausted.
There are no easy exits from the middle phase of grieving. But gradually the intensity of the emotions subsides, and the mind is once again able to take control through faith.
If you're still in the struggling phase, experiencing a deep confusion and wondering about your sanity or your orthodoxy, please take heart. What's happening is not strange. You haven't lost your mind. You haven't committed the unpardonable sin. You're doing what Job did (see Job 3–39), striving on many levels—with God, with his friends, and within himself—for peace, reconciliation, wholeness.

Regardless of all the pressures from your friends, your spouse, or even from within yourself to act, speak, or feel in some more orthodox way, my advice is this:

- Be truthfully yourself.

Do not pretend. Do not lie. But look your struggle in the eye, whenever you can, with help if you need it. And slowly—as slowly as necessary—come to terms with it. All the while remember that your life is in God's hands, and that he understands your struggle and is far more patient, gracious, and forgiving than you can ever imagine.

If you want to be healed, in his way and in his time, he *will* bring the healing you need. The final phase is deeper faith, a renewal of trust, a more realistic and balanced view of God's way in the world. Best of all, you may emerge, like Job, with a more personal relationship with God: "My ears had heard of you but now my eyes have seen you" (Job 42:5). This is what I wish for you, more than anything else.

But this positive resolution is not inevitable for anyone. And no one else can choose for you. So, Jesus asks you again, "Do you want to be healed?"

After all, there *are* some advantages to keeping things the way they are. Your depression, despondency, and despair are effective ways to remind everyone of your loss and to keep yourself unhappy, which you may think is all you really deserve, considering what happened. And your sadness does elicit sympathy, even pity, something you wish everyone would feel for you.

When you think it through, though, wouldn't you rather have their love than their pity? Wouldn't it be wonderful to have those relationships healed?

Are you willing to forgive those who have tried to help for not always knowing just the right thing to say or do?

They can't meet all your needs anyway, so why not stop expecting them to?

Only God can.

One more biggie: What about yourself? Can you forgive yourself for being just a human being, no pillar of the faith, just little old you? For hanging onto your pain for all this time? For hurting all this time, and being lame instead of healed already, etc., etc.?

I'm *not* asking you to forget.

You couldn't even if you tried.

But you *can* work with God to redeem it all for good. From the very beginning, I knew what he wanted me to choose. I wrote in the journal, "I thought we had carried enough already, but evidently not. Why? Why not? God's plan [must be] to use us . . . to redeem this."

God wants to do the same with your pain. Remember: your pain is mine, and mine is yours, but the best thing is that *our* pain is *his*. Jesus bore the cause of our pain at Calvary, and someday he will eliminate suffering altogether.

But for now, God extends us—you and me—the privilege of turning our losses into gains, our pain into power, for his kingdom. As Paul put it,

> Praise be to the God and Father of our Lord Jesus Christ, the Father of compassion and the God of all comfort, who comforts us in all our troubles, so that we can comfort those in any trouble with the comfort we ourselves have received from God.
>
> 2 Corinthians 1:3–4

That's his plan. And your journey toward wholeness must inevitably lead you along that path—away from despair and into the joy of comforting others, bringing them his peace.

But before we continue, I need to tell you something important about this chapter, in fact, about everything you've read so far.

The process of resolving grief is not a straight line, a continual progression from the pits to the peaks. In reality, it's more like a spiral, or perhaps a series of successes and failures. If you charted it on paper, it might look like a graph of the stock market.

Perhaps you are not quite ready to process what I've said in this chapter. Perhaps it produced anger or resentment, when you thought we were getting along so well. If so, would you try to find yourself somewhere in these first few chapters, and start walking again?

There's no rush.

The rest of the process can wait.

But if you're ready to continue, the next few chapters aim to help you build a more solid faith for the days ahead.

My brother Paul, a general contractor, sees an analogy between how he builds a house and how God builds us. When it's time to get underway, Satan—the excavator—digs a big, deep hole. The digging tears up the landscape, ruins the view, and generally make a mess of everything.

The excavator's plan is to throw us in and bury us.

But when that hole is just the right size, God—who has been watching closely—steps in and says, "Okay, that's enough. It's just right." And he begins to pour the foundation for the dwelling he's had in mind all along.

When **LOSSES** Come, **WHAT** Do I Know?

6

God Loves Me

I Can Count on Him

KNEELING BEFORE THE dead child's mother, the Christian doctor tried to help. "God loves you," he offered.

Eye to eye, she responded, "I hate God."

Here are two more lessons from the University of Pain:

- The first principle is that God loves you.
- The second principle is that pain's laboratory experience seems to contradict principle 1.

Survey the horizons of life—truthfully. Look beyond the trifles, trivialities, diversions, and amusements and gaze upon the naked truth:

Out, out brief candle! Life's but a walking shadow, a poor player that struts and frets his hour upon the stage and then is heard no more. It is a tale told by an idiot, full of sound and fury, signifying nothing.[1]

Perhaps you prefer a more orthodox source:

I, the Teacher, was king over Israel in Jerusalem. I devoted myself to study and to explore by wisdom all that is done under heaven. What a heavy burden God has laid on men! I have seen all the things that are done under the sun; all of them are meaningless, a chasing after the wind.

Ecclesiastes 1:12–14

Or, hear the words of Moses, reviewing his life:

All our days pass away under your wrath;
we finish our years with a moan.
The length of our days is seventy years—
or eighty, if we have the strength;
yet their span is but trouble and sorrow.
for they quickly pass, and we fly away.

Psalm 90:9–10

The horizons of life do not demonstrate God's love. Instead we see troubling things.

Pain
Frustration
Competition
Alienation
Disintegration
Decay
Death

Yes, even the death of a child, perhaps our own child. By itself, does such a loss lead me to conclude that God loves me and has a wonderful plan for my life? Not hardly, although a realistic survey of the evidence that life provides may *drive me* toward the Father, longing for the comfort of his love. But my own needs, regardless of their intensity, provide no reliable information about *him*. Need-fulfillment is very much like wish-fulfillment—a flimsy foundation for trustworthy theology.

How can I know, then, that God loves me? Do my role models show it? Sometimes . . . sometimes not.

> I used to climb a big tree by our house and look around to see if he (dad) was coming. (I really didn't know that there was a lot more world than I could see from that tree!) It was while sitting in that tree one day I realized that he was never coming home. It felt as though something had actually broken inside my chest. I've always been afraid of being abandoned since then. It's hard to believe or understand God and all his promises—I don't mean that I don't believe at all, but it's hard to understand the love of God when you've missed out on the love of your dad.[2]

Sadly sometimes our earthly fathers do little to reinforce the belief that God, our heavenly Father, actually does love us. So we look for love in all the wrong places, and we end up with visions of God that did not originate with him:

- The Big Stick—just waiting for an opportunity to beat on you some more.
- Sugar Daddy—collecting your requests for more trinkets and toys.
- The Iceman—removed, cold, and aloof, despite all your attempts to get closer.
- Mr. Wizard—able to magically fix all your problems.
- Shoulda-woulda-coulda-oughta-mighta Judge—cannot be pleased no matter how hard you try.

Christian teaching and personal advice tend to focus primarily on corrections in the mind and will, while virtually ignoring emotional scars that may also need healing.

Wendy is a sincere, intelligent Christian woman who has known the Lord for many years. Besides being a housewife and mother, she graduated first in her class from nursing school and is considered extremely capable and dependable in a hospital setting.

For several years, however, she had been struggling with a deepening depression—not "spiritual" or intellectual, but linked to her inability to *experientially know* the love of God, because the love she had known as a child was so conditional.

> Looking back, trying to find an answer, grabs at the inner, deep feelings and emotions, wrenches like a cut of a sharp object into a very tender area; sharp, stinging, then dull and aching. It is choking me, cutting off my air-supply. My head feels, physically, as if it is on fire under my scalp. I have a sensation of impending doom. . . .
>
> I hurt, yet I don't want to ask for help. I must get help; somehow I have to reach out and admit my need or end my life.
>
> I want to live, though; somehow I need permission from within myself to go on living.
>
> I know God loves me. I know I need the fullness of his love. But do I dare accept it. . . .
>
> I am afraid to accept God's love for fear of rejection, most of all.
>
> Do I want to believe in God? Do I dare to trust him? I don't know.
>
> P.S. Lord, let me experience the joy of your salvation. Please! I want to believe.

Left to ourselves, we might *never* reach the conclusion that God loves us. In fact, based on the evidence, other conclusions seem more likely. And even if we do decide we really are loved, our pain—like Wendy's—may stand in the way of that belief becoming an experiential reality.

The good news, though, is that discovering God's love is not entirely up to *us*. God wants to be known as he is—a loving heavenly Father to all who are part of his family by faith. This was at the core of Jesus's revelation about God, especially to those religious "experts," the Pharisees, who were so caught in legalistic self-righteousness that they had no vision of the Father's mercy, compassion, lovingkindness, and grace.

The apostle Paul (a former Pharisee himself) gave a remarkable affirmation that the faith relationship enables us to come to God as our "Abba," the common Aramaic childhood term of endearment, which in English is "Daddy."

Our loving Abba-Father, God—patient, understanding, kind, and wise—wishes to be known, but we have to look in all the right places:

> But God demonstrates his own love for us in this: While we were still sinners, Christ died for us.
>
> Romans 5:8

"Look at the cross," the apostle was urging, "and you will know in your *mind* that God *must* love you."

Look. See. Understand. Perceive the love of God demonstrated in ultimate terms—a truly convincing, convicting appeal to the mind, and many have come to repentance through its message. "God loves *me*! It cannot be denied. He proved it at Calvary."

Beyond Ideas to Experience

Notice the larger context of Romans 5, and another appeal, here summarized: we also know his love in times of distress, for it is then that God pours out his love into our hearts by the Holy Spirit, whom he has given us (see Rom. 5:1–5). In other words, it is *especially* in times of trouble that we come to *know* something about the love of God. The Greek word used here for *know* means to have seen or perceived. When used of God, it means absolute knowledge, and when used of us, it means to know by observation. In times of distress, God is there, living within me in the Person of the Holy Spirit, who whispers in my pain, "I love you." And I come to know that truth in my *heart* as well as in my mind.

I carried on an extended conversation with Marian, the mother who had asked, "What's wrong with me?" as she struggled with the pain of her daughter's death. Almost the first thing I wrote to her was this:

> If I could summarize what I would want you to know, I would put it like this: GOD LOVES YOU. GOD LOVES YOU. GOD LOVES YOU! And he loves [our children] more than we do. Can you REST in that? Can you cease striving and KNOW it? I trust that you will one day be able to say, with a settled conviction, I KNOW IT with a knowledge that is both intellectual AND emotional.

At Calvary, Jesus proved his love for me. As I ponder the suffering of Christ, and wonder that he chose, as my redeemer, to shoulder pain beyond my comprehension, I glimpse the *heart* of God.

In eternity, when God will be free to reveal—and I more able to comprehend—the height and depth and length and breadth of his love, and how the time and seasons, joys and sorrows, flowed together in a harmony I sometimes could not hear, I will know the *mind* of God.

But in the now of my life, when I'm hurting and struggling, wondering and wandering, groping and even griping, that is when I look into the *face* of God and his love becomes for me more personal, more practical, more real—just when I need it most.

This kind of *knowing* is hard to explain or describe— something like an intuition, but much more credible—a knowing that involves both mind *and* heart, yet super- cedes them both. I have perceived his love in a special way through suffering.

But how? It seems a rather schizophrenic claim.

And why is suffering such a unique classroom for these lessons of love? I asked my friend and fellow pilgrim Dr. Edward Kuhlman what there is about suffering that proves God's love. Here is his response:

> PROVE is a big word. . . . For some people (perhaps most) suffering is incontrovertible evidence (proof) that God doesn't love them! I think the proof issue has to be established first, and for me, in part at least, it concerns the *very* nature of God. (What do I know about the na- ture of God???)
>
> Anyway, I see God as The Suffering God. Increasingly I'm led to the conviction that God is profoundly *feel- ing.* . . . To suffer is to touch the skirts of God's Being. Did not Jesus say, "I am meek and lowly in heart" and that implies tremendous vulnerability. . . ?
>
> Beyond that, I think God's sensitivity necessarily in- volves suffering. Creation does not give us the true picture of God's Being (I am fond of saying). Redemption alone does! Love leads to (requires? without being perverse or masochistic) suffering. The *sine qua non* of love is pain—suffering.

After more than a decade in my personal wilderness, I now know more of the love of God, a perception of divine reality that can best be gained, perhaps can *only* be gained, at the University of Pain.

First, I know he loves me because *he is here,* in the midst of my struggle, sharing the pain. I am not left alone in my effort to understand, or merely survive. He did not create this universe just to send it spinning through eternity at the whim of fate. Nor did he create this individual—me—and call me to himself only to leave me on my own to understand this riddle—life.

Because he is now here, I am not fatherless, an orphan, abandoned, without support or guidance, nurture or protection. Amazingly, the apostle Paul affirms that because by faith we have been adopted as children of God:

- We are spiritual brothers and sisters of Christ.
- We are full-heirs of God and joint-heirs with Christ.
- We have already been raised up with Christ and seated with him in the heavens.

See Romans 8:15–17; Galatians 3:26–4:7; Ephesians 1:3–14; 2:4–10.

Now, as my loving father, God is far more concerned with my developing character and maturity than *I* will ever be. So, as he lovingly oversees the events of my life, he sometimes allows experiences that will bring out the best in me when, if I were the master of my own destiny, I almost certainly would choose another course. This parallels the process of human discipline that proves parental love (see Heb. 12:1–13).

Because he is now here, I am not comfortless. Jesus promised the Holy Spirit's presence as one who would comfort, guide, empower, convict of sin, and bring glory to him (see John 14:16–27; 16:5–16). Like a mother or nurse, the very Spirit of God, who resides in me by faith, comes alongside as someone who listens, speaks, prays with me and for me, even when I cannot find words to express what I truly feel (see Rom. 8:26).

Because he is now here, I am not an only child. I have a friend, closer than a brother, who understands the path I walk because he has walked it too (see Heb. 4:14–16). His heart beats with mine. His heart breaks with mine. His hands reach out, through their own pain, to touch my aching soul and let me know that someday it will all become clear—but for now to keep on walking, like he did and like others have before me.

For I have other brothers and sisters who walked the path of faith—sometimes conquering kingdoms, shutting lions' mouths, quenching the flames, escaping the sword . . .

> whose weakness was turned to strength; and who became powerful in battle and routed foreign enemies . . . others were tortured and refused to be released, so that they might gain a better resurrection. Some faced jeers and flogging, while still others were chained and put in prison. They were stoned; they were sawed in two; they were put to death by the sword. They went about in sheepskins and goatskins, destitute, and persecuted and mistreated—the world was not worthy of them. They wandered in deserts and mountains, and in caves and holes in the ground.
>
> These were all commended for their faith, yet none of them received what had been promised. God had planned something better for us so that only together with us would they be made perfect.
>
> Hebrews 11:34–40

See Hebrews 11:1–12:3 for the larger context.

Even today I have many brethren in Christ's body, the Church. I cannot adequately express what their support has meant to us—emotionally, spiritually, financially, and in many other practical ways. Beyond that too is the shared wisdom of the Church: godly writers and teachers helping fellow pilgrims find the passes through the mountains of pain.

Second, beyond God's family, he has given me his Word—something solid in turbulent times, a topographical map that shows the guides where to look for these passes. Space prohibits listing the passages and the promises that provide wisdom to understand the ways of God with man and give hope and strength for the journey. Numerous books have organized and systematized the helpful promises of God. Perhaps one may be written that will compare the relative space given in the Word to faithfulness *in* suffering to escape *from* it, which seems the goal of some popular "theology."

My personal expectation is that for every verse lifted out of context to support the "gospel of health and wealth," fifty can be found exhorting faithfulness in the now as we expectantly long and look for the coming glory. Jesus summarized this perspective in these simple but profoundly realistic words: "I have told you these things, so that in me you may have peace. In this world you will have trouble. But take heart! I have overcome the world" (John 16:33).

Third, I have also learned that through suffering, God can show us who we really are, fortifying our present hope. As Paul said, "We rejoice in the hope of the glory of God. But we also rejoice in our sufferings, because we know that suffering produces perseverance; perseverance, character; and character, hope" (Rom. 5:2–4).

Hope of what? That I really am God's child. That he really is my father, my brother, my friend. Haven't you wondered about that? After all, considering your doubts, your fears, your questions, your angry protests, how could it possibly be true that *you* are a child of God? The evil one would love to bury your hope in a coffin of doubt.

But, for his own purposes, God has *chosen* to allow you to pass through this refining process. And like the steelmaker, God does not just dig up any old dirt and throw it in the smelting pot. Not even the highest quality mud makes it to the fire. Only ore—the real thing, authentic raw material—is good enough for that. As Job said, "When he has tested me, I will come forth as gold" (Job 23:10).

When God is through refining you, the same will be true. Looking back, you will see the kind of person the fire has refined, and you'll know why the Lord has invested so much in you, one of his own, and in that quiet confidence there is hope. If he believes in you, perhaps it is safe for you to do the same.

And finally, I have seen how his redeeming love rescued me from an almost abject helplessness in the face of pain far greater than I could endure by myself. Helplessness may be our greatest fear, and it is certainly our greatest frustration. Satan will do all he can to nail us to the cross of helplessness. And then—as he must have done at Golgotha—rejoice with diabolic glee.

But Satan is not all-powerful. He is not all-knowing. He is a created, limited being. Although he has great power in this world, greater is he that is in me than he that is in the world (see 1 John 4:4). It is especially in times of difficulty, as we cry out in our helplessness, "Lord, help," that Almighty God steps in and turns it all around—helplessness to power—for him.

Several days after Christopher's CT-scan shattered my life again, I was taking a shower and reflecting on the direction our path had suddenly turned when I focused my anger on the evil one, saying something like this: "Satan, you b_____, you can't have this one. Satan, you're going to be sorry."

Not that I've had extended conversations with that pretender, nor do I make it a point to personally challenge the personification of wickedness. In fact, in Jude 9, we're told that even the archangel Michael did not bring a slanderous accusation against Satan, but said, instead, "The Lord rebuke you!" That is what I should have said. However, this was a turning point for me, because it helped me concentrate my anger on Satan as the tormentor rather than on God—and somehow I knew that this time the result would be different. In fact, when

I first started working on this book, I was calling it, "The Christian Phoenix—Power from Pain."

This power is not from myself, not something I produce on my own, or I will surely fail, leaving myself and those I love at risk in this warfare. It is *not* something that can be achieved—as some secular writers encourage—by steeling the will, but only by humbly linking my helplessness with God's power, my weakness with his strength.

It is another of those remarkably consistent paradoxes of faith. To some this may seem foolishness, and to them it may be—the same "foolishness" as the foolishness of the Cross, which confounds the wisdom of men, "For the foolishness of God is wiser than man's wisdom, and the weakness of God is stronger than man's strength" (1 Cor. 1:25; see 1:18–31).

No man's strength could overcome the power of death, and no man's wisdom could provide a certain way to God. But in the person of Christ, and at the place called Golgotha, God accomplished both. Through the weakness of Christ, I am strong. Through the death of Christ, I am alive. Through the stripes of Christ, I am healed. Through the resurrection of Christ, I see God's power to make things right in the end. So even if today life seems to be a living hell, through him I have a living hope.

7

Suffering
Has Value

I Can Trust Him

Dateline: China, circa 1967
The eighty-year-old grandmother, lame for many years, is driven down the town's main street, head half-shaved, face painted, sign hung around her neck. At the sound of the gong, she is forced to announce her crime . . . "I am a Christian."

The children grab at the soldier's leg, begging for an end to this abuse. "Be quiet, children . . . be quiet," she says. "I've been waiting for years for the chance to testify to my village like this."

Dateline: U.S.A., circa 1987
"I see no point in suffering," the wife of a once famous TV preacher announced. And many American couch-Christians probably nodded in agreement.

The gospel of health and wealth, a vain self-deception, has given birth to a generation of spiritual pygmies, powerless pretenders longing for protection from life's harsher realities. For them, suffering is when the extra Mercedes is broken down or the dishwasher isn't working or the grocery store has run out of kiwis. . . .

Painless suffering is a modern phenomenon, perhaps linked to the developments of modern science aimed at eradicating disease and alleviating pain. Until very recently in history, people expected pain and knew how to live with suffering. Just envision life without aspirin—much less Valium—and no anesthetics.

Today, with so many medications and treatments available, we've come to expect a fairly pain-free life, even while dying. "Just a little more morphine, please. And if perhaps it seems I may have to pass through the valley of pain, please take me away, Hemlock Society."

So, the modern mind has trouble finding a place for pain in the ways of God with man, unable to see the value in suffering. As Peter Kreeft aptly wrote,

> But if the most important thing in life is conquering suffering and attaining pleasure, comfort, and power by man's conquest of nature, then Jesus is a fool and a failure. . . . And the society that makes the relief of suffering its *summum bonum* does not understand the meaning of suffering or of pleasure.[1]

Suffering is a major theme of the Scriptures, and integrally intertwined with redemption, the overarching theme of God's Word to man.

Man Suffers

A *Time* magazine article about life in the Soviet Union spoke of Russian wisdom: "A sense that in life grief flows continuously in and out of happiness, and happiness in and out of grief."[2]

Creation Suffers

> The creation waits in eager expectation for the sons of God to be revealed. For the creation was subjected to frustration, not by its own choice, but by the will of the one who subjected it, in hope that the creation itself will be liberated from its bondage to decay and brought into the glorious freedom of the children of God.
>
> We know that the whole creation has been groaning as in the pains of childbirth right up to the present time.
>
> Romans 8:19–22

God Suffers

The Father, from eternity past, carries the sorrow of the sacrificed lamb—his only begotten Son—mingled with the joy of the lamb's redeeming work, even as the foundations of the world are laid (see Rev. 13:8).

The Son, as he walked among us, suffered with us and sorrowed over us. He wept at the tomb of Lazarus. He wept over Jerusalem, longing to bring his people back to God like a mother hen gathers her chicks. He was touched with our infirmities and moved with compassion over our needs. He struggled against temptation, and he agonized in the garden until his sweat became like drops of blood. And on the cross, beyond the physical suffering, Jesus encountered the agony of the outer darkness as his Father turned away from the sin laid on him, the iniquity of us all (see Isaiah 53).

The Spirit suffers with us, pouring out God's love in our hearts and providing comfort, wisdom, guidance, and power in difficult times. He expresses our deepest longings in groanings to the Father, and he is grieved when we return to godless patterns of communication or conduct (see Eph. 4:30).

Suffering Is Everywhere

Suffering is in us and around us. To pretend otherwise is to deny both reality and revelation. And suffering is part of the curse, the old order of things that will someday pass away in the great reversal and renewal of realities (see Rev. 21:1–5).

But within the context of faith, suffering has value:

> Love somehow goes with suffering. Freedom goes with suffering. Truth, wisdom, knowledge of reality, go with suffering. It seems that everything that has intrinsic value, everything that cannot be bought or negotiated or compromised or relativized or reduced, goes with suffering.[3]

In other words, suffering can be a significant occasion for growth, for at least five reasons.

The first value of suffering is that it helps eternal realities break through. Wisdom is to see realities as they are, and to know how to function most fully, productively, and constructively within these realities. In times of distress, God breaks into our temporal existence and helps us see more clearly. In his extended comparison of temporal and eternal realities, the apostle Paul affirms both sides—that pain is pain in our present reality, but in the light of eternity, pain is a tool that God is using to prepare us for a reality greater than we can imagine this side of heaven.

> We are hard pressed on every side, but not crushed; perplexed, but not in despair; persecuted, but not abandoned; struck down, but not destroyed. . . .

Therefore, we do not lose heart. Though outwardly we are wasting away, yet inwardly we are being renewed day by day. For our light and momentary trouble are achieving for us an eternal glory that far outweighs them all. So we fix our eyes not on what is seen, but on what is unseen. For what is seen is temporary, but what is unseen is eternal.

2 Corinthians 4:8–9, 16–18; see 4:1–5:10

One morning I was called to the scene of a fire where six children and their mother had died. Three of the children had been in the children's choir of the church I pastored in Michigan's Upper Peninsula. After walking among the rubble, viewing the charred remains, my vision of realities was sharpened. The starkly grotesque scene of destruction confronted me with the frailty of temporal life *and* the true significance of the eternal.

Thankfully, the eternal—the life that emanates from God—is bigger, able to swallow up the temporal—what we usually regard as "life"—"so that what is mortal may be swallowed up by life" (2 Cor. 5:4).

In the mind of God, there is only one reality, his reality—whether it is seen from this side and labeled "mortal" or from his side and called "life." At all times, we live and move and have our being in him.

Prosperity whispers that we are creating our own destinies, but suffering shouts that the only way to overcome our frailty is to allow it to be linked to his finality by faith.

A second value of suffering is that *God's Word can take on more personal meaning*. For example, in Isaiah 55, I am invited to come with empty hands, wounded heart, and confused mind in response to his gracious invitation: "Come, all you who are thirsty, come to the waters and you who have no money, come, buy and eat!" (v. 1).

Through the lens of loss, I see that most of my energy has been unwisely expended pursing happiness, a fleeting temporal dream. Exhausted, or perhaps bankrupt, I turn to God seeking a more lasting satisfaction. Listening to him, I become a more discerning consumer, able to know what is good, so that my soul delights "in the richest of fare" (v. 2).

Facing distress greater than myself, I may wonder how I will ever survive. Depression saps my hope, joy, and peace. But faith still hears, "Give ear and come to me; hear me, that your soul may live" (v. 3). And faith still seeks the Lord, turning to him for mercy and pardon, and trying to understand his ways (see vv. 6–7).

But sometimes his thoughts and ways are not what I would choose (see vv. 8–9). Why do bad things happen to good people? Why do good things happen to bad people? Why do good things happen at all? The latter questions are as valid as the first. Bad things happen because sin has permeated this world, and good things happen because God is gracious, to the unjust as well as the just. If good things happened only to God's people, then everyone would want to claim that identity, and "faith" would be just one more way of manipulating him.

As to bad people and good, there is evil in everyone, and the only good person is the Lord. Fortunately, through my faith, my sin has been laid on him (see Isaiah 53) and his righteousness on me, so that whatever he allows or causes in my life cannot be for judgment but for discipline—a process of becoming more like him.

"Tragedies" are events, yes, but they are also part of a process, as are rainstorms and snowstorms (see Isa. 55:10). As events, they may be helpful or harmful depending on their intensity, but as part of a process, they have a purpose.

God's Word is like that too (see Isa. 55:11). His message to me often comes in the context of events. (What are you saying to me in this, Lord?) Sometimes I hear, and sometimes I cannot discern, but even then I can still trust, because I always know that his Word cannot fail to fulfill its purpose, so his purpose in my life cannot fail.

This purpose is always positive, constructive, and redemptive, versus the consistently destructive plans of the evil one. Results include joy and peace, song and celebration (see Isa. 55:12–13), a transformation of realities as the eternal breaks into the temporal, and all for the everlasting glory of God.

Third, *my suffering links me to Christ by faith*. One unmistakable message of the early Church was "If you identify with Christ by faith, expect to suffer for it." This is exactly the opposite of a popular philosophy that says, "If you identify with Christ by faith, expect to prosper for it."

A Christian doctor was struggling with the specter of a second malpractice suit, wondering if he would survive this one, even thinking of retiring from medicine (which would be an even greater tragedy, considering how few Christian doctors there are). Medical school did not prepare him for this pain, affirming instead, almost from the outset, "You are the chosen ones, the elite, the privileged few."

Perhaps Christ is saying,

> You are *my* chosen one, standing with me, the great physician as a healer of the whole person. My way is the way of the cross, to be unjustly accused, judged, even convicted, so that by my stripes you may be healed. *Our work* is to risk this pain to counteract the intentions of the evil one, to struggle against the suffering that came into this world through the curse. As one who is dying, you will work to mollify the pain, and postpone the dying of the rest.

Millions have embraced the privilege of sharing in the sufferings of Christ—the continuing sufferings of Christ—that came to them because they said they belong to him. The apostle Peter wrote,

Dear friends, do not be surprised at the painful trial you are suffering, as though something strange were happening to you. But rejoice that you participate in the sufferings of Christ, so that you may be overjoyed when his glory is revealed. If you are insulted because of the name of Christ, you are blessed, for the Spirit of glory and of God rests on you. If you suffer, it should not be as a murderer or thief or any other kind of criminal, or even as a meddler. However, if you suffer as a Christian, do not be ashamed, but praise God that you bear that name.

1 Peter 4:12–16

Do you belong to Christ? If so, and especially if you have made that fact known, *expect* suffering. The evil one is concerned to destroy your testimony, to undermine your witness, to sap your strength, to steal your joy.

But don't despair. As with Job and Peter, and countless others who have walked the path of faithfulness, God may allow your path to pass through pain. But his purpose is always for good, in us and through us, and he never lets us walk that vale alone.

In Philippians 3:10, the apostle Paul speaks of "the fellowship of sharing in his sufferings, becoming like him in his death." Somehow through identifying with Christ in my sufferings, I can gain a new appreciation of the path he chose, more freely than I, and I can also learn something of its cost.

Since by faith I have linked my life with his, my pain is his and his sufferings are mine. Therefore, it matters little what the source is, nor how intense the pain. What matters most is whether or not I can give it to him, letting him control and transform it for his purposes and even for his glory, and in the process I can discover fellowship with God that I never knew before. As Peter Kreeft explains,

84

What then is suffering? It is Christ's invitation to us to follow him. Christ goes to the cross, and we are invited to follow to the same cross. Not because it is the cross, but because it is his. Suffering is blessed not because it is suffering, but because it is his. Suffering is not the context that explains the cross; the cross is the context that explains suffering. The cross gives this new meaning to suffering; it is now not only between God and me but also between Father and Son. The first *between* is taken up into the Trinitarian exchanges of the second. Christ allows us to participate in his cross because that is his means of allowing us to participate in the exchanges of the Trinity, to share in the very inner life of God.[4]

The fourth value of pain is that *it can become a special platform for witness to others.* Heroic suffering, the faithful witness of a special few, encourages the rest of us to keep walking, while exhorting us to be strong and courageous. How many handicapped persons (as well as those without a physical handicap) have been inspired by the witness of Joni Eareckson Tada, quadriplegic artist-singer-actress-author-speaker, etc., who through giving her pain to God was able to see him transform it for his glory?

Or consider this translated letter from the wife of an East Asian pastor, imprisoned for his faith and now blind because his captors confined him in a completely dark cell.

It is pitiful to see him still being confined in [a] dark cell with no light. But his powerful spirit still remains and bears much fruit for the Lord.

As for me and our two children, since the day we were put out of our residence at the church, we have been wandering from place to place for survival. . . . Presently, for the past two months we have been staying out on a balcony. But I thank the Lord and gladly accept everything he permits to come into our life, trusting that he provides us with sufficient strength to endure. I know the Lord has a good plan for our life. In adversities, trials, suffering we can see how marvelous are the Lord's blessings and joy. The Scripture in Isaiah 25:4 gives me much comfort and encouragement to stand firm in my faith in the Lord, not to become fainthearted, but to step forward facing all circumstances.[5]

Suffering is an opportunity to learn to trust him. For me, this has been the biggest value, and the hardest struggle. How many times have I gone into my children's rooms at night to listen for their breathing, sometimes putting my hand on their chest to be sure they *were* breathing, trying to look an unspeakable fear in the eye, knowing the only answer is trust?

Edward Kuhlman's book, *An Overwhelming Interference*, took its title from this quote of A. W. Tozer:

> One picture of a Christian is a man carrying a cross: "If any man will come after me, let him deny himself, and take up his cross, and follow me." The man with the cross no longer controls his destiny; he lost control when he picked up his cross. That cross immediately became to him an all absorbing interest, an overwhelming interference.[6]

The crucial question is this: Having taken up the cross, am I now willing to trust the one who controls my destiny? Do I welcome his cross's interference?

Just a few days after Christopher became ill, I was walking outside the hospital with a good friend, and I expressed my frustration something like this: "You know, God has us by the throat"—though later Edward Kuhlman suggested that God has us by the *heart*! It was my way of voicing my combined fear, helplessness, and resentment of God's interference. Do I trust him? My cynical self says, "There's nowhere else to turn. I'm trapped, without options, and totally at the mercy of my maker."

My faithful self says, "Yes, I do trust him, but sometimes it's not that easy."

For instance, after more than nine years of searching for medical answers to our sons' illnesses, we finally connected with a physician who offered a succinct four-sentence explanation of what had happened to our two boys.

It was good to finally find an expert resource in relation to this rare condition, but this physician's letter was also a source of fear, since it implied that Christopher might later face a similar crisis, under certain adverse conditions. It is possible that our girls, if not personally at risk, may be carriers of this genetic defect. So, not only do we live every day in fear in the present generation, but assuming our girls do survive to adulthood and marry, we will never be quite free of anxiety should they have any children of their own.

This same physician enclosed a copy of an article linking blindness in adolescence to a similar disorder, which threw me into severe depression as I wondered what he might be trying to tell us, or prepare us for. The unknown can produce an overwhelming fear, especially when the known has almost destroyed you.

How do you handle fears like these? You just keep walking—walking by faith, believing:

- He knows enough to understand what's happening.
- He's powerful enough to work it all for good.
- He's kind enough to respect your limits.
- He's loving enough to forgive your doubts.
- He cares enough to calm your fears.
- He's gracious enough to accept your faith, weak as it is.[7]

8

Jesus Wants
Me Whole

Alive from the Inside Out

FRIENDS TELL EACH other the truth, and the truth is, friends, we can't let go. There is only one reality that we would accept. There is only one reality that would relieve this pain:

• To have things just the way they were before.

That's the reason for years I kept, in an airtight container, a rose I plucked from atop Jonathan's casket in 1978.

That's the reason you still have your daughter's bicycle, when she's been gone these many years. And you still haven't been able to redecorate her room or dispose of her clothes and toys.

It's why your son's achievements and character development somehow always fail to measure up to what she would have produced . . . if she were still here. And perhaps it's the reason that just the other day, he protested, "I feel like I'm always competing with my dead sister."

It's why your neighbor visits her husband's grave every day and why she can't seem to go anyplace in town without talking about what she and George did there.

Maybe it's the reason you don't go to church anymore, or if you do, there seems to be a block between you and your former friends, the pastor, or even between you and God.

Why can't things be the way they were?

Why did it have to turn out this way?

If only you had known more, or done things differently.

If you hadn't gotten so caught up in your work, perhaps she would have stayed.

If you had just taken a different road that day.

Why did you let her go out with that group to that place?

If you had just been more alert to the symptoms.

Maybe a different diet would have helped.

If only you'd had enough faith.

It's so terribly hard to accept what's happened. I long for things to be the same, don't you? Wouldn't you give almost anything for just one more year—a month, a day—of having things the way they were? To walk with him one more time along that quiet wooded road, or watch her run happily across that mountain meadow. . . .

And that is how we feel, in spite of the fact that we know in the deepest part of ourselves, this one fundamental University truth:

- Nothing stays the same.

Everything changes.
Everyone changes.
You, yourself, have changed.
If you had him back, you would even find that he has changed. Ask any spouse who waited so long and faithfully for her POW husband to return.

Ask any bereaved parent why the marriage ended not long after the child died.

The fact is this: the reality we long to regain exists only in our imaginations. Every effort and all the energy invested is wasted. Like poor Humpty, all the king's horses and all the king's men could never put our life together again. And even if they could, our highly selective memories of the way we were would provide inaccurate blueprints for the reconstruction, and the pieces would never fit anyway.

But, oh, how we try, we each in our own way. Sometimes the pursuit of that illusion leads down shadowy, scary pathways of depression, even institutionalization, as the demand to have what cannot be becomes the central focus in a fantasy world.

But, you protest, if I were God. . . .

Ah, there's the real core of the problem. From Adam to this very day, the desire to be gods has kept us captive to wellness versus wholeness. Wellness is health and wealth, long life and happiness, by our own definition.

If I were God, I would never have done it that way. The way I would do it might go like this: The righteous would prosper and the wicked would suffer. There would be no birth defects or genetic diseases. In fact, there would be no diseases at all, especially diseases like cancer, or Alzheimer's, and AIDS. There would be no injustice, famine, or pestilence. Everyone would have enough, and the innocent—especially innocent children—would never suffer, and certainly, they would never die.

But if upon further consideration I decided upon a less radical return to Eden—allowing some of these atrocities to exist in the world of my creation—I might preserve the first equation and allow them to plague only the ungodly. For everyone else, there would be an escape—the out of faith. Inhabitants of my world would be able to avoid its pain by believing and practicing righteousness.

Sound familiar? The "gospel" of health and wealth bombards the airwaves night and day, leading its disciples into a very subtle servitude—slavery to the little tin gods who masquerade as masters of faith. "If you will only have enough faith, or the right kind of faith. If you will only claim the promises and link yourself to the power . . . our power. . . ."

If only you were God. . . .

This approach ultimately fails when the rubber meets the road and God's ways diverge from ours. Theme-park theology collapses when bad things happen to good people, but the roller coaster keeps running for the sad disciples, who are now in a worse state than before. Not only have they failed to receive what they desired, but their "teachers" have left them the almost inevitable deduction that the reason for that failure must lie in their own weak or nonexistent faith, or perhaps in some unconfessed sin.

While their adherents languish in pain, these pretenders strut and fret about their respective stages, pontificating and pronouncing what God must do—when the truth of the matter is that God must do nothing, except remain faithful to himself and his Word. In reality, their pronouncements represent just what they would do if they were God.

Jesus wants you whole, whether or not you are well. Whether or not you are well is his concern too, but only a temporary issue. Wholeness has value for this present life as well as for the life to come.

The fact that wellness is temporary (or you could call it temporal) is obvious when you take a God's-eye view and see that all flesh is grass—here today and gone tomorrow. What we call "life" is like a mist in the night, a candle that burns awhile in the darkness and then fades away.

What is usually called "health" is, itself, an illusion. In Western cultures today, the word's usage implies the absence of obvious physical symptoms. If the doctor can't find anything wrong with you, you are therefore in good health. But we all know of vigorously "healthy" athletes and others in good "health" who have now gone on before us.

The gospel of health and wealth, when all the hype is stripped away, is simply an extension of humanistic thought, values, and goals, a twentieth-century search for the fountain of youth. Eradicate pain and suffering, extend life, postpone death, control the environment—control everything—take the place of God. And at its heart, like the secular humanism it fails to recognize as its own father, this "gospel"—which is no good news at all—certainly cannot embrace the value of pain and suffering in God's grand redemptive plan.

When we focus on wellness, we simply cannot see the whole picture. When I started organizing my thoughts for my doctoral work on personal wholeness, I thought that the answer was inner healing or the "healing of memories," but that was a reflection of my personal needs at the time. Before long I began to see that true wholeness is far bigger than that, a central theme in Scripture, at the heart of the meaning of redemption, and the key to the fullness of life and joy that knowing Christ can bring.

By contrast to modern formulas, which may be profound to the point of obscurity or simplistic to the point of absurdity, God's way to wholeness is both simple and profound at the same time.

On one occasion, for instance, Jesus reduced the essence of divine revelation to two commandments:

> Love the Lord your God with all your heart and with all your soul and with all your mind. . . . Love your neighbor as yourself.
>
> Matthew 22:37–39

Personal growth toward wholeness is possible, thank God, but the wellness it requires is relational, not situational. To have a present and increasing love relationship with God, self, and others is its simple, yet profound, condition. The result is reconciliation and peace, a whole-person impact—body, soul, and spirit.

Many Christians have not considered the possibility that their sometimes vague sense of fragmentation is not necessarily a "spiritual" problem, because unspirituality seems to be the only answer they hear. And there is some truth to it, after all. For illness in one area *must* impact all the others. So, it *is* a spiritual problem. But its true root may be somewhere else, perhaps in their nagging sense of alienation from others, even from their own selves.

Like their Creator, they are a special unity in diversity. They are one person, certainly, but also body, soul, and spirit. Just one unwhole component and the entire harmony is broken. Spiritual Band-Aids may bring temporary relief, but fragmentary repair jobs produce fragmented people.

What we're all longing for—wholeness—is a small taste of redemption, which is really our effort to recapture the perfect wholeness known before the fall. Its memory is all but erased, but still there, in our heart of hearts. All religions touch on this theme somewhere: reconciliation, serenity, peace—man seeking God, even man seeking to become God.

But all man's seeking and striving for that redemption must end in frustration, because the key lies not in seeking but in being sought—God seeking man, longing to provide through faith in Jesus Christ what all of us desperately lack without him. And it is through accepting as a gift what we cannot achieve on our own that the primal reconciliation begins. Its result is life—from the inside out—bringing more than wellness, even more than wholeness, the possibility of holiness.

I asked Edward Kuhlman how wholeness is better than wellness, and he provided his usual unique perspective:

> Let me suggest this—there is a third factor that transcends both and ties the two together—HOLINESS, the Old English word for health (holth) implies both—wholeness (togetherness) and wellness. God clearly is more concerned with wholeness (integrity would be my term—hence JOB's commendation). When the layers are peeled away, do we find anyone home?

Wholeness does not ignore our need or desire for physical wellness. Good health is a gift from God, an expression of his common grace to all—or even his special gift to me, when through a divine intervention, he brings healing and restoration through someone he has endowed with a special gift. Or perhaps he may heal me without any intermediary. He is remarkably creative in his methods of healing, as demonstrated in the ways Jesus healed.

But good health, as commonly defined, is not the greatest good; wholeness is. Actually, the glory of God and the extension of his kingdom are truly the greatest goods. But since we're talking here about personal implications, his kingdom's coming into our lives brings the possibility of wholeness, and that wholeness finds its ultimate expression in the extension of his kingdom to others, which brings glory to God.

Physical healing isn't even the greatest healing miracle. There are many healings, but the greatest is the healing of spirit and soul that comes from reconciliation with God through faith. Recognizing our need for a savior, we turn to God by trusting in the saving work of Christ, turning away from our sins, and placing our lives in his control.

But if, by his choice and in his way and time, God chooses to miraculously restore a person to physical wellness, the only appropriate response is joy and worship.

So we pray for physical healing, believing that God *can* heal, and hoping that he *will* heal. Yet we are willing, if his answer is "No," to let him be God, his will be done, his kingdom come. And we invite others who are gifted by him to pray with us.

But we never "lose more than we have to," as one pastor remarked in a seminar I was leading. Our lives and our times are in God's hands. No intellectual, philosophical, emotional, or theological pyrotechnics will ever change that. What is required of us is faithfulness and trust.

When the prophet Daniel's friends were threatened with being thrown into the fiery furnace if they would not bow down to Nebuchadnezzar's image, their response was

> O Nebuchadnezzar, we do not need to defend ourselves before you in this matter. If we are thrown into the blazing furnace, the God we serve is able to save us from it, and he will rescue us from your hand, O king.
>
> Daniel 3:16–17

This is where the name-it-and-claim-it preachers often stop. But this trio's perspective is more balanced and realistically faithful as they continue, "But even if he does not, we want you to know, O king, that we will not serve your gods or worship the image of gold you have set up" (Dan. 3:18).

Sometimes, our God chooses not to rescue us from the furnace of affliction. The power to do so is his, but his present intervention at our request does not serve his larger purposes.

A Lutheran pastor wrote, in relation to the fact that his own brother was not healed at his request, that God's answer seemed to be something like, "I'm sorry, I can't." This is the same kind of answer that Rabbi Kushner gave in his book *When Bad Things Happen to Good People*. But our God is never powerless, except to violate his own character and Word. His answer is never, "I can't."

In fact, in relation to his promises, God's answer is always "yes" in Christ, according to the apostle Paul:

> For the son of God, Jesus Christ, who was preached among you by me and Silas and Timothy, was not "Yes" and "No," but in him it has always been "Yes." For no matter how many promises God has made, they are "Yes" in Christ. And so through him the "Amen" is spoken by us to the glory of God.
>
> 2 Corinthians 1:19–20

But what of the times when his answer so obviously seems to be a resounding "No!"? For instance, when our friend Janet Gilson prayed one December day that God's angels would surround her son Brent's car, she had in mind her twenty-year-old son's safety. It was a prayer she often prayed, but how could she have known that Brent would die in that car that very night, a victim of a drunk driver? "Where were the angels?" she would ask of God. How could a Christian mother's sincere prayer be denied so absolutely? Only with the ear of faith could Janet hear, "They came on a different mission—to carry Brent to the arms of Jesus."

If we were God, we would always say "Yes" to events that contribute to the kingdom plan. The problem for us, since we are not God, is that we *cannot know* all aspects of his sovereign plan. And if we could, how would we hope to remain objective, much less kingdom-controlled in relation to ourselves or especially those we love? Given control over our own destinies, we would often—if not always—choose the way of health and wealth, when God's design might require something very different.

So, sometimes his response—which is always "Yes" in relation to his larger purposes and his faithfulness to the promises—can sound like "No" to us. (For further discussion of this, see the second half of chapter 11.)

But can we say "Amen"—so let it be—through Christ, anyway? Paul did, after *pleading* three times that his thorn in the flesh be removed:

> To keep me from becoming conceited because of these surpassingly great revelations, there was given me a thorn in my flesh, a messenger of Satan, to torment me. Three times I pleaded with the Lord to take it away from me. But he said to me, "My grace is sufficient for you, for my power is made perfect in weakness." Therefore I will boast all the more gladly about my weaknesses, so that Christ's power may rest on me. That is why, for Christ's sake, I delight in weaknesses, in insults, in hardships, in persecutions, in difficulties. For when I am weak, then I am strong.
>
> 2 Corinthians 12:7–10

Having heard directly from the Lord that his power—the "Yes!" Paul was seeking to change his situation—is perfected in weakness, the apostle wisely chose to *delight* in weaknesses, for in knowing how weak he was, he could learn something of the strength of Christ.

This is the paradox of the Cross. The Savior, perfect God/perfect man, submits himself to brutal humiliations, and a cruel, excruciating, agonizing death. He chose a fragmentation that involved his total self: body, soul, and spirit.

Stop the action, freeze the frame at Calvary, and the verdict would be "Satan wins. Evil is triumphant. Life is meaningless madness. Let us eat, drink, and be merry, for tomorrow we may die." But, of course, the drama didn't end at Calvary. It continued past Easter including the post-resurrection appearances and revelations. It even continues today, as Christ has been raised up and is now seated at God's right hand, where he intercedes night and day for the brothers and sisters who long to see his face, and even to perhaps experience on this side of heaven some sense of the realities of glory. Wholeness now, integration, joy and peace, power in our weakness, while confidently expecting a more perfect wholeness then.

Wholeness is a *present* reality in the mind of God. Through faith in Christ, we stand complete, lacking in nothing. When the Father looks at me, he sees the righteousness of Christ, the courage of Christ, the strength of Christ, the character of Christ. I am—already—an heir, joint-heir with the son, an eternal member of the family circle (see John 1:12; Rom. 8:17; Eph. 1:13–14).

Wholeness is a *future* reality that I claim now by faith. For I know that when I see him, I will be perfectly whole, finally like him, able to truly reflect his glory, and always delighting in the "Yes" of his will (see Rom. 8:13–23; 2 Cor. 4:16–18; 1 John 3:2).

Wholeness is a *progressive* growth experience in this life that involves my entire person: spirit, soul, and body. As God's presence within gives me life, this new life is expressed in improving relationships with God, myself, and others. In this pilgrimage, my goal is to become more like Christ, whose character is developed in me and expressed through me by the Holy Spirit (see Rom. 8:28–30; 2 Cor. 3:18; Gal. 5:22–23; James 1:2–4).

One of the greatest errors of the health and wealth perspective relates to confusing the *already* and the *not yet* aspects of redemption. Already we can be *becoming whole*, even when God's ways diverge from ours. Handicap, illness, or deformity cannot hinder wholeness, except in the mind of men. But to affirm this, our definitions of wellness and parameters of "defect" must be brought into line with God's, who always looks at the heart and is far more concerned with who we are and who we are becoming than whether or not we are "well."

Sometimes, the greatest wholeness may even come in the last weeks or moments before death, when the heralds of health and wealth have turned away in disgust or derision. One young physician—a mother to ten—expressed this kind of wholeness, as recalled by one of her daughters:

> In terms of hope and "will there be life again" I have to thank Mom for her incredible help in preparation for life after her death. For someone who had never died before, she did everything perfectly the first time. Our conversations and plans for the remainder of my life combined with my hatred of the pain she so uncomplainingly bore have made this time after her death one that is not crippled by grief. I am busy and excited about getting back to school and social activities. And I know that that is what Mom would have wanted. She told me a few weeks before she died that even if she wasn't dead by summer she wanted me to leave—go to school or just live in a city with friends and have fun. Her exact words were, "One semester is long enough to put your life on hold." She was right—I am re-entering my life (it really seems like I had a sabbatical) and am having a lot of fun (something I haven't had a lot of these past few years).[1]

This dying mother was a more integrated personality than some will ever be. Certainly, she must have hated the disease process that was stealing her life and future earthly joys. Certainly many people prayed with her and for her that God would miraculously intervene. Although he did not intervene in the way they all might have wished,

100

his grace was obviously sufficient, and his power was evidenced through her weakness.

When the apostle Paul speaks of delighting in weakness, he has made a conscious choice to embrace God's way with him. This is one of the most crucial components of moving beyond the inevitable difficulties of life toward wholeness, usefulness, even power for God. It is the exact opposite of the natural response most of us make, at least for a while—refusing to let go, striving with everything inside us to cling to the past somehow.

The pathway through the mountains of pain inevitably passes this point. Am I ready yet to embrace God's way with me?

A choice to hold out or hold on takes me back into the mountains again. But the conscious decision to let God be God, to give up the demand to have things just the way they were, and to embrace his way is the beginning of integration. For embracing his way is the pathway that leads to embracing him—the one trustworthy foundation for reconstructing my fragmented self.

It's a scary choice, sometimes reached only after wandering for months, or even years. But it is the only way I know that leads away from the guilt, remorse, anger, bitterness, depression, and even despair, which can enslave me to the past. And it is the only road that leads toward life, and love, and even joy.

Instead of waiting for things to return to as they were, accept where we are and wait to be even better.

When **LOSSES** Come, **WHO** Do I Know?

9

Loving God
in a New Way

Loyalty

"HOW CAN I convince my son he doesn't need to be afraid?" the old man wondered.

Tied atop the altar like so many ritual sacrifices he had observed, Isaac looked into his father's eyes. "How can this be happening?" he asked himself. His father loved him so and had spoken so often of his miraculous birth.

"Oh, Lord," Abraham prayed, looking away. "Is it possible I have misunderstood your command?"

He strained to hear the voice he'd heard so often before. But there was only silence and the sound of the wind on the mountain. Deep within him a personal storm raged.

The events of the past few years flashed through his mind, a mixture of regrets, joys, failures, and successes. But overshadowing everything else was *the promise*—and Isaac, the son he loved more than life itself.

Watching him die would be like witnessing his own execution. But, he reasoned as he took up the knife, if the Lord God had done one miracle to bring Isaac into the world, he could do another now, if need be—even to the point of bringing him back from the dead!

Faithfulness and Love

Abraham's test is one of the Bible's most dramatic incidents (see Gen. 22:1–18). Ordered to offer Isaac as a burnt offering, the father of faith complied, to the point of taking up the knife, before God intervened, providing instead a ram as a substitute.

There are many lessons here, but the clearest thing is that God put Abraham to a test (see Gen. 22:1; Heb. 11:17–19).

It was a test of loyalty.

Did Abraham love Isaac more than he loved God?

It was a test of faith.

Could he be obedient beyond reason, giving the son back to God with only his word to go on?

He decided it was worth risking. Weighed in the balances, he was found faithful.

I never had Abraham's choice. Without comment, Jonathan was whisked away, and I was left to try to sort things out. Had I been given this choice, only God knows how it would have gone.

At one point, I came to the conclusion that I had loved Jonathan more than anything—even God. One observer suggested that perhaps that was why God took Jonathan away. I didn't consider that possibility, but decided that kind of God wasn't the one I knew.

With time, I've come to see that the problem wasn't that I loved our son too much, but that I loved God *not enough*. As C. S. Lewis explains:

> It is probably impossible to love any human being simply "too much." We may love him too much in proportion to our love for God; but it is the smallness of our love for God, not the greatness of our love for the man, that constitutes the inordinacy.[1]

Burnt Offerings

In Abraham's story, God's provision of the substitute ram is one of the Old Testament's more obvious symbols of what he would do for us through Christ at the cross, where the Lord offered himself in our place.

But Satan loves to deceive us. He seems especially adept at using our confused emotions (notably guilt) in times of distress to tempt us to atone for our own actions, regardless of what Christ accomplished at Calvary. He wants us to become prisoners to the past, convicts in the courtroom of our own heart, sentenced to self-imposed unhappiness and pain. For years, because I was hurting so deeply, I allowed *myself* to become a burnt offering, consumed by the fires of anger turned inward (which brings depression) and anger toward God suppressed (which becomes bitterness). Only through the help of several friends was I able to let it go, although reluctantly at first.

I recall praying and weeping with one friend at a church in Maine. With another I visited Jonathan's grave, after having stayed away for five years, praying there a prayer of thanksgiving for ever having had our boy to know and love. But even after that many years, and several cathartic confessions, I can still recall Bill's statement as we approached the Cornish-Windsor covered bridge, "Then it's not really over yet, is it?"

It hurt to hear it, but it was true. I knew God's pathway leads toward joy, but perhaps it was because I didn't want to become well that the healing took so long. I didn't want to let go, and holding onto the pain seems to be one way to hold onto the person. By contrast, to begin to enjoy life again can seem so disloyal.

Was I hoping to become whole without actually dealing with the rage? My depressed mind whispered that gradually I was recovering, lifting *myself* out of the "slough of despond."

Depression is such a deceitful state of mind.
Little rays of hope seem like beautiful rainbows.
Is this momentary happiness the beginning of joy?
An hour's serenity seems like the start of a lifetime of peace.

But then the painful memories crush these passing fancies into the pit of despair and I wonder if this sadness will ever cease.

The truth is this: only God could lift me from that pit. Only he can bind up the brokenhearted. If only I could be reconciled with him, I could be healed. But it's a doublebind, approach-avoidance problem. Needing his touch, I have to resolve my anger first, perhaps something like this:

God, I'm angry at you. I don't like what has happened. I wish things had been different. For all these years, I've held you responsible—and maybe you are responsible.

In any case, right now, at this moment, I do forgive you. By that I mean that I am releasing my resentment, anger, and bitterness, recognizing it has kept me in slavery to the past. I will no longer dwell on this event in my futile efforts to change the past or to get back at you.

And, Father, I thank you for your forgiveness. I will no longer punish myself, nor will I allow Satan's deception to put me back on that altar when I know that Christ has already paid the penalty for all my sins.

Lord, I know that holding this in for all this time has hindered our relationship and my effectiveness for your kingdom. I turn away from those destructive emotions now, and toward you again, thanking you for your understanding, patience, and love. Cleanse me, O God, and let me know again the joy of your salvation. More than anything else, I want to be closer to you, and I want a sense of your being closer to me.

Then, when my love is tested, however it happens, I will be able to turn to you, my friend, look into your eyes, draw upon your strength, and turn away from whatever or whoever it is—because I love you more. Amen.

Forgiveness, Reconciliation, and Relationships

We *can* forgive God because he is a personal being as we, made in his image, are personal. We *must* forgive God because the only true way to interpersonal reconciliation is forgiveness. In fact, the only way to resolve the defiling pain of bitterness is through forgiveness.

Some may be uncomfortable with this approach, and I'm not absolutely sure of it myself. My emotional self says, "Yes," while my mind says, "How can God ever need to be forgiven?" But then, isn't this inner tension of divine versus human perspective at the center of the continuing divine-human encounter in the trysting place of pain? And is it possible that this way of describing this human-divine interchange is like the Old Testament passages where God repented or changed his mind? In other words, perhaps this concept is more useful in describing the result (in this case, reconciliation) than it is in defining the process, which may be somehow beyond human language.

I'm using Lewis Smedes's idea of forgiveness here. He says, "When we forgive, we transcend the pain we feel by surrendering our right to get even with the person who hurt us. But there is a judgmental side to forgiving: no one ever forgives a person without blaming him first."[2]

Am I suggesting that we judge God? May it never be, though we may be tempted to do so. Job was tempted to do so: "Then know that God has wronged me and drawn his net around me. Though I cry, 'I've been wronged!' I get no response; though I call for help, there is no justice" (Job 19:6–7).

I cannot be God's judge, first of all because I'm not qualified, and second because my faith accepts and affirms that by definition he is both loving and just, so his actions cannot be otherwise.

But do we blame him?

Be honest.

We do.

So "forgiving" God may be the most effective way to remove the bitterness, restore the fractured relationship, and declare our willingness to let God be God, even in the situation that brought our pain.

Now I'm not suggesting that you *should* be angry at God if you're not. Nor am I encouraging you to blame God if you're not already doing so.

Usually, the blaming or bitterness is not a conscious thing anyway. It happens automatically and is so quickly repressed that most believers don't even know such destructive feelings have gripped their heart. For instance, this is what happened to a person I'll call John Peterson:

As he scooped his dying son from the crimson snow, John Peterson saw the color slowly fade from the boy's face. The sledding accident never should have happened. It was senseless, tragic, a loss he could not have imagined, and the beginning of an inner fragmentation he could not now control as he watched the child's life slip away.

This fragmentation was not immediately apparent, either to John or to his friends, for hadn't he arranged all the funeral details and handled himself through it all with such courage? Hadn't he even witnessed to others of how the Lord was sustaining him?

But it was there. Cradling the dying boy in his arms, and overwhelmed by the force of the event, John Peterson had turned *to God* and *away from God* at the same instant, and it wasn't until several years later that he even became aware that his anger had become bitterness, hindering his relationship with God and blocking the movement toward wholeness that he so longed for and needed.

There is a John Peterson in every pew of every church in our land, someone who has experienced fragmentation on a deep level, who now struggles with the unresolved pain. We pain-aholics know intuitively that this is true, but the more scientific among us look for proof. The primary symptom of this defiling reality is the common struggle to truly love God with our whole heart.

For years, I struggled to build the kingdom (with some success), but something was wrong. My efforts lacked heart. I could not love God while hating so intensely something he had allowed. Our fractured relationship required repair, reconciliation, and renewal through the process of forgiving and being forgiven.

This is the real problem with suffering, but one that is sometimes missed even by authors quite sensitized to the issues involved. Consider the following passage from *The Strong Name* by James Stewart:

> Right at the outset let me say this—that if there is one subject in which the use of any language that is merely facile and conventional must be reckoned as a positive offense, it is this subject of the mystery of suffering. . . . Stock phrases, for instance, like "the nobility of pain," "the uplifting influence of suffering," are very easy to use, but may simply prove that the one who uses them has never grasped what the real problem is. Would you go to someone in trouble and say to him piously, "Ah, but

friend, consider how good this is for your character"? Would you try to heal his wound with tags of commonplace counsel like "Take courage; it might have been worse"; or "Don't worry: it may never happen"; or "It's a long lane that has no turning"? All that may be true enough; but it has scarcely begun to come in sight of the real problem, and it is certainly not within shouting distance of the Christian answer. The one thing that is quite inexcusable in this whole matter is to be complacent and platitudinous. For when we approach this mystery, we are treading on holy ground.[3]

What then is the *real* problem in suffering? For James Stewart, the question, "How, seeing it *has* happened, am I to face it?" is deeper than, "Why has this happened to me?" He argues, "The New Testament is . . . desperately and magnificently concerned about How? It does not offer you a theory and an explanation; it offers you a power and a victory."[4]

But for me the "real problem" in suffering is not philosophical (Why?), or practical (What am I to do?), or even a question of power (How am I to face this?), though with the last one we're getting closer. The greatest questions in suffering—for the serious believer—are *relational*: relationships with God, self, and others.

The greatest question in relation to God is "Am I or am I not going to remain loyal to a God who works in my world in this way?" It may take a while to resolve this, as it did with Job, but the process has great potential for growth. As Edward Kuhlman wrote to me:

Now the time is propitious to KNOW God and to know myself and to know myself [in relation to] God—the time is pregnant—it is a birth of sorts. Can I shed outdated, worn, no longer appropriate notions . . . and grow into God? Call it reconciliation—it is relational, you're right. Otherwise the whole thing is useless. Why do I need to learn HOW [i.e., How am I to face this?]

112

in that way? Why the bother? Why the bathospheric burden that threatens to drown me. . . . Just so God can say to Satan or anyone else, see I told you he'd do it! Job had to be not only better but DIFFERENT as a result of the trial.

Growing Closer to God

Jesus taught that the commandment central to all the rest is "Love the Lord your God with all your heart and with all your soul and with all your mind" (Matt. 22:37). It's my settled conviction, based on almost forty years in the Church, that many Christians seek to fulfill this commandment through tireless service. But the sad fact is that many have been serving God for years without heart because their deepest God-ward feeling is resentment rather than love.

Perhaps one reason Chuck Colson's book *Loving God* was such a best seller (besides the excellent writing and gripping illustrations) is that many believers realize, when they stop pretending, that they have not been able to fulfill this crucial command from Christ. Yet even Colson's effort to inspire us to consider this central issue, "how to love God," needs to go one step further.

Colson states that loving God involves fulfilling these seven callings: belief (faith in God through Christ); repentance (recognizing the reality and awfulness of personal sin and turning away from it); obedience (without regard to the cost) to the new Master; holiness (developing godliness in character, motive, and action, with emphasis on personal discipline); "binding up the brokenhearted" (ministry to the outcast and downtrodden and concern for justice); service; and seeing the world as God sees it.

What I would add is that instead of trying to discover *how* to love God, or even to *prove* that they love God, many believers should ask themselves first *if* they love God.

Do You Love Me?

It is possible to serve God from *fear* as readily as from love, without others being able to discern true motivations. Ultimately, only God knows. I may even deceive myself by my quantity of activity or sincerity of desire to please him.

Since the dawn of revelation, man has judged by externals and God has looked at the heart. The greatest commandment *does not* find its fulfillment in external righteousness today any more than it did in Jesus's time. This was among the Lord's most significant messages, and if he were preaching here today he would deliver it again: "The issues of life flow from the heart. True obedience flows from love, and not the other way around. The first question is not, 'Are you obeying me?' or even 'How are you showing that you love me?' but '*Do you love me?*'"

Starting in the Wrong Place

The danger of starting in the wrong place is that twentieth-century orthodoxy can be as dead as the first-century variety, providing a false security and an inappropriate superiority—faith without heart. The self-satisfaction created can keep me from realizing that in my heart I nurture not much love toward God.

Love without action is not really love, but no amount of activity can ever prove that I really know and love God. Unless the things I do for him are my humble expression of adoring appreciation for what he has already done for me, my good works can become ends in themselves—a

114

source of pride, convincing me that since my works are good and right, I too am good and right.

The true servant knows better. As our Lord taught, "So you also, when you have done everything you were told to do, should say, 'We are unworthy servants; we have only done our duty'" (Luke 17:10).

Starting in the Right Place

> How do I love Thee? Let me count the ways.
> I love thee to the depth and breadth and height
> My soul can reach, when feeling out of sight
> For the ends of Being and ideal Grace.
> I love thee to the level of every day's
> Most quiet need, by sun and candle-light.
> I love thee freely, as men strive for right;
> I love thee purely, as they turn from praise.
> I love thee with the passion put to use
> In my old griefs, and with my childhood's faith.
> I love thee with a love I seemed to lose
> With my lost saints—I love thee with the breath,
> Smiles, tears, of all my life!—and, if God choose,
> I shall but love thee better after death.[5]

Poets, musicians, writers, and painters have all tried to capture the sublime qualities of human love. Yet, if we know God, we also know that the best of human love is still but a pale reflection of Love himself. Why is it, then, that we are so poorly prepared to use such language or concepts in describing how we love God? Notice, the poet does not say, "You know I love you, don't you, let's count the ways." Or, "How can I prove I love you, let's think of some ways."

"O God, my God, how I do love Thee, let me count the ways. Let me try to describe my love. Let me use analogies to speak of its qualities, its height, depth, length, and breadth—its strength, and its grip on my heart."

Which of these ideas describe your love for God?

Appreciation	Communication	Commitment
Loyalty	Faithfulness	Trust
Honor	Openness	Friendship
Desire	Cherish	Fondness
Respect	Intimacy	Communion
Pleasure	Adoration	Complete when
He is first	Closeness	with him

Could you write a love song to God?

> I love you, O Lord, my strength.
>
> Psalm 18:1

> My soul yearns, even faints,
>   for the courts of the Lord;
> my heart and my flesh cry out
>   for the living God.
>
> Psalm 84:2

> I love the Lord, for he heard my voice;
>   he heard my cry for mercy.
>
> Psalm 116:1

> As the deer pants for streams of water,
>   so my soul pants for you, O God.
> My soul thirsts for God, for the living God.
>   When can I go and meet with God?
>
> Psalm 42:1–2

> Then I will go to the altar of God,
>   to God, my joy and my delight.
> I will praise you with the harp,
>   O God, my God.
>
> Psalm 43:4

Can you sing a love song to God?

> Sing to the Lord a new song;
> sing to the Lord, all the earth.
> Sing to the Lord, praise his name;
> proclaim his salvation day after day.
>
> Psalm 96:1–2

> I love you, Lord, and I lift my voice,
> To worship you, O my soul, rejoice;
> Take joy my king, in what you hear,
> May it be a sweet, sweet sound in your ear.[6]

Can you *feel* a love for God growing in your heart?

Learning to Love

After twenty years of marriage, I love my wife, Ann, much differently now than when we first met. Such adolescent emotions and commitment could never have sustained us. My expectation is that a significant part of our remaining years together will be invested in nurturing our love toward even greater maturity. It will take work, energy, and time together. Relational growth requires pain. It's not easy. But the value of living and being loved is almost beyond articulation.

Learning to Love God

We grow in our love relationship with God too. In the beginning, it may have seemed so simple. He loves me and I love him. How could anything improve on that? Now if I can learn his expectations and obediently fulfill them, everything should go happily ever after.

But after that honeymoon expires against the brick wall of reality, the possibility of a deeper relationship begins.

Some people become disappointed, angry, resentful, or bitter. Others may compliantly accept whatever comes their way.

My own typical response has been to hammer it out, adjusting my expectations and even my categories, as the Lord has walked me through this life. Where once I had a more intellectual approach to faith, now my perception is that he is right here with me, longing for the same communion and relationship I so desperately need as we pass this way together.

As in marriage, I have a covenant relationship with him. It's been tested and I've been tempted, but that commitment still stands, and at its heart is a growing sense of loving him.

> O Lord, my Lord, how I do love thee,
>   let me try to count the ways.
> I love thee as a child his father,
>   trusting as he learns and grows;
> Or as a lamb might love the shepherd,
>   following wherever he goes.
> Or is it like a flower the sunshine,
>   or as the fawn must love the doe?
>
> And sometimes we are paint and artist,
>   clay and potter, poet's song.
> For you are making something lovely
>   even when things seem so wrong.
> I wish to love as bride her husband,
>   in passionate fidelity,
> Or as disciple loves the master,
>   reverential loyalty.
>
> But mostly we have been companions
>   on a path without an end,
> And I have come to love you fondly,
>   pilgrim—partner, friend to friend.

10

Toward Integration

Real People in a Plastic World

SLOWLY THE TERRORIZING memories came to the surface in the cauldron of Connie's disintegrating pain. Years of psychotherapy had brought her to this point. Gradually she had been able to recall long-submerged childhood incidents of physical, emotional, and sexual abuse by both parents. Now, with horror, she saw herself being forced to participate in the Satanic ritual murder of a newborn baby. Is it any wonder Connie had experienced a fragmentation of self known psychiatrically as multiple personality? Yet by the grace of God, and through the help of her therapist, this young woman has been finding integration around a new personal center, Jesus Christ.

I hope your tale of personal fragmentation is not as appalling as Connie's, though stories like hers are becoming far more common than most people would expect. And I trust the results of your disintegration were far less destructive to your psyche. But at some point, reality bashed your earnest expectations to smithereens. You were left to piece the fragments together again somehow, like poor Humpty of nursery rhyme fame. And "all the king's horses, and all the king's men"—friends and lovers, parents and pastors, counselors and others—tried to help. But all their efforts and words, their ideas and suggestions, could not ease the pain.

Linda wrote to me about trying to deal with her young son's death:

> My faith and concept of God was shaken—not torn down—but shaken. I'm struggling to understand. I know I must be obedient and trust him no matter what. I am looking forward to the good that the Lord will bring out of this loss—but I must confess it seems that nothing could be worth the loss of our beautiful baby. I am aware of most all that God has revealed in his Word—his ways are not mine . . . but I still hurt.
>
> You really expressed my feelings when you said you can't hold, kiss, hug—a biblical truth. I know God's promises are true but at this point it doesn't ease the pain and it seems it should.[1]

In this kind of storm, when hope lies shattered and broken on the ground, philosophy, psychology, theology, formulas, and disciplines may all become part of the healing process. But what Linda needed most was a *person*, a person who understood and cared, who wouldn't judge her doubts or criticize her truthfulness, who would accept her unconditionally, hear her lament, weep with her until *she* was ready to stop, share her pain, then gently whisper, "Peace. Be still. And when you're ready to go on, we will."

I speak, of course, of him who "was despised and rejected by men, a man of sorrows, and familiar with suffering" (Isa. 53:3).

Letting Jesus into Your Pain

Are you ready to let Jesus into your pain?

"But 'Nobody knows the sorrow I've seen,'" you answer.

He knows.

"And no one has suffered my agony."

He has.

"Can anyone feel the pain I feel?"

He can.

"But no one can mend a broken heart."

He will.

But first, some things will have to change.

In fact, *everything* will have to change, because if you let Jesus into your pain, it has to be on his terms. He wants to rebuild your realities from the center outward. He's not content to stay on the fringes of your faith. He must be Lord.

The control of a model airplane on a tether is in the hands of the pilot. Dips and doodles, takeoffs and landings, are all governed by subtle movements of the wrist and hand.

If the plane could think, it might have a different perspective! "How well I glide, twist, and turn. I just wonder how well I could do, all by myself. I have the power, I have the aerodynamics, if only I could be free. I could fly off into the sky and have such a wonderful time!"

If the plane could will, then it might be able to work itself free, only to discover that without the tether, without the pilot at the center, a crash would be inevitable.

Perhaps this is similar to what William Butler Yeats had in mind when he wrote,

Turning and turning in the widening gyre
The falcon cannot hear the falconer;
Things fall apart; the centre cannot hold;
Mere anarchy is loosed upon the world,
The blood-dimmed tide is loosed, and everywhere
The ceremony of innocence is drowned;
The best lack of all conviction, while the worst
Are full of passionate intensity.[2]

When God made man like himself, it was to have un-fettered fellowship and relationship with him. In fact, before the fall, there was a perfect harmony: God and man, man and woman, humans and their world. But when sin entered, it brought alienation on every level: man and God, man and woman, man and nature. A hideous disintegration began, from that place and time ever outward to the entire universe, which even now could be heard groaning in pain—if we had the ears to hear it—longing for the renewal.

Something died that day, as God had warned. It was man's capacity for perfect fellowship with the Creator, because where once there was holiness at the center—a spirit alive to God and subject to his desires—now there was another nature, tainted by sin with all its pride and arrogance. Man had become self-centered. Only through faith in God's promise that One would come to make it right again were our first parents able to have a restored relationship with their maker.

How like the story of our own lives! Self-centered from the very moment we arrive in this world, our life becomes increasingly dominated by arrogance and pride as we seek to create meaning and find fulfillment by our own efforts, without any lasting success.

We long for more, for a different and deeper reality than we can find in this world. In our collective mem-ory we retain the sense that true harmony is possible, as Augustine reminded us, "Thou hast formed us for

Thyself and our hearts are restless till they find their rest in Thee."[3]

What has to happen is renewal, actually rebirth. We were born physically, but as Jesus explained to Nicodemus (see John 3), if we want to see the kingdom of God, we must be born again of the Spirit. As with Adam, so with us, this rebirth occurs through faith in Christ. At our invitation, he actually takes up residence in us (see Rev. 3:20), bringing his transforming life into the very core of our being.

To understand this process, I like to compare the nature of man to an egg. The danger in any comparison that divides our essential unity is that one or more components might be overemphasized, at the expense of the rest. Or possibly the true sense of the larger whole will be lost—like dissecting a frog to discover how it's put together only to find that you've killed it along the way.

But the apostle Paul speaks of our whole spirit, soul, and body being kept blameless at Christ's coming (see 1 Thess. 5:23). So to understand what it means to be transformed, inside to outside, through Christ's coming to our lives, let's use the analogy of an egg.

First there is the body, the shell, the external self that everyone can see. But that is not the only self, nor is it the real personality, which most of us are able to realize intuitively the very first time we go to a funeral. The shell remains, but the person we knew and loved is gone.

If we peel an egg (hard-boiled), within the shell we find the egg—"the essential reality of eggness," the philosopher in us might say. Behold the soul: the mind, will, and emotions that are an individual's true and eternal personality. Surely these develop and hopefully they mature. But this is what you will take with you into eternity when it's time to go, at least temporarily, until at the resurrection, you are reunited with your resurrected body and are truly whole again.

But wait, if we look inside even further, we find the egg yolk, the central core, the life force of the egg itself. Likewise, within us, in the center of our soul is the spirit, the life force if we know Christ, or the source of decay and death if we don't. When we receive Christ as Savior, his Spirit penetrates our personality to the very spirit core, bringing life where there was death, renewal where there was decay.

But our own nature is not destroyed. It is not eradicated by his presence, nor is it absorbed into him. It retains its egocentric orientation, its desire to be in charge. Thankfully now, at least, we do have hope and we do have life, although the struggle between the old and new ways can sometimes be intense (see Romans 7). And the basic issue always remains: "Am I willing to grant control to him, or will I insist on doing it my own way? Who is at the center at this very moment?"

This brings us to one of pain's graduate-level lessons:

- The old center has collapsed, and I am helpless.

Pain gives you new eyes, eyes to look beyond these temporary things we normally label "life" and see into eternity. And now you have new ears as well to hear his voice. Your mind is sensitized to understand, and your will is ready to respond. But most of all, by coming to the end of yourself, you have learned this most difficult of lessons, the folly of integrating life around anything other than God. As Francis Schaeffer said, "There is only one integration point that is enough, and that is God himself."[4]

Perhaps your center was material things, and now they're gone. Or it was good health, and that is threatened. Or maybe it was another person—your son or daughter, wife or husband, or someone else you loved very dearly—and now that person is gone. Or maybe it was friendship, and you have been betrayed. Or fame, and you have been defamed. Perhaps it was career or intellectual pursuits, or maybe it was even theology or ministry. Whatever it was, if it took the place of God as the central focus of your life, the house had to fall (see Matt. 7:24–27) because nothing other than God can ever be enough.

If it was your *self*—your own abilities, strengths, knowledge, and wisdom, your own egocentric values and perspectives, and your own control—and now through pain you've learned that center "cannot hold," rejoice! For Jesus said, "If anyone would come after me, he must deny himself and take up his cross and follow me" (Matt. 16:24).

Actually, this radical renewal on Jesus's terms requires three stages: self-denial; death to self; resurrection to life in him.[5] Our part is to deny that we, ourselves, are worthy centers of our own universe and to center instead on Christ, who invites us to "take up the cross" with the same intention and intensity he did—to die on it—or to lose our life for his sake (see Matt. 10:39).

His part is to give us the meaning and fulfillment we long for—"to the full" (John 10:10).

When I first entered the ministry, I chose as my "life verse" Philippians 3:10: "That I may know him, and the power of his resurrection and the fellowship of his sufferings, being conformed to his death" (NASB). I wanted to know him. And I wanted the power. I even wanted the fellowship. But, when I chose that verse, I had yet to learn that knowing him (which comes from fellowship with him) could come *only* from sharing in his sufferings. The resurrection power only *follows* conformity to his death, and there's nothing that kills you like the suffering or death of your own children.

So, in the beginning, I chose to share in his pain, not knowing what that choice would mean. But in the process I learned that the only way I could survive was to share my pain with him, because otherwise it is a burden too heavy to bear. And having learned my weakness, another section of Scripture has taken on special meaning:

> But we have this treasure in jars of clay to show that this all-surpassing power is from God and not from us. We are hard pressed on every side, but not crushed; perplexed, but not in despair; . . . struck down, but not destroyed. . . .
>
> Therefore, we do not lose heart. Though outwardly we are wasting away, yet inwardly we are being renewed day by day. For our light and momentary troubles are achieving for us an eternal glory that far outweighs them all. So we fix our eyes not on what is seen, but on what is unseen. For what is seen is temporary, but what is unseen is eternal. . . .
>
> Meanwhile we groan, longing to be clothed with our heavenly dwelling . . . so that what is mortal may be swallowed up by life.
>
> 2 Corinthians 4:7–9, 16–18; 5:2, 4

Seeing the Way He Does

Most of us live primarily by sight and not so much by faith. We are oriented and integrated around temporal things. But when by faith we give our pain to him, we can have a way of seeing that is more eternal than temporal. On learning of his second bout with cancer (the first was thirty-five years earlier) David Stewart, M.D., sent out a letter. I have excerpted it here with his permission:

> Here are some specifics to add to your prayers for me and others in similar situations:
>
> • For a stable mood. Moods can be slippery and unpredictable at times like these.

126

- That I not try to intellectualize my situation. Reason offers little leverage on cancer. I've always had an affection (not a talent) for reason but here it's futile. Faith if fertile. . . .

  fear it (handwritten)

- And pray for my own faith, that it be stronger, pertinent, coherent, contagious.
- Pray that there will be no sham, no pretense, no posturing, no glibness, no superficiality, no focus or dependence on what I am or can do, but only on Christ.
- And I'll join you in praying for those others who need healing or relief or safety more than I.

. . . A great privilege it is to live in our soiled and risky old world, to share in the grime, the aches, and the unlove, yet still to know love, to know joy even as we accept the consequences.

. . . There is much we'd thought yet to do; we're inclined to do it still and, with a renewed awareness, give him credit for each moment. Surely we'll find an answer in all this somewhere.

But just now we are content. These days are satisfying, even exciting. I'd trade places with no one.

Because he has allowed Jesus to enter his difficult situation, Dr. Stewart can see beyond the now and into eternity.

So, are you ready now to let Jesus into your pain? If you are ready, you may want to pray something like this:

Dear Jesus,

I can see now that I've been trying to carry this heavy burden by myself—and I've failed to miserably. I have been trying to put the pieces back together, but nothing seems to work. And now I understand that you are the only one who can help, that nothing else and no one else can be the foundation for rebuilding my life.

So now, right now, I give my life to you—pain, disintegration, and all—expecting that with you at the center,

127

in your way and in your time, you'll make some sense of it.

Lord, you know how lonely this has been and how isolated I've become. It just seemed like no one else could understand and no one really cared. But I do believe that you are with me now as you've been with me all along, and that you understand the way I feel. Thank you, Lord,

And thank you, too, that through this pain I've felt a part of what you felt when you walked in our world. Because of that I can experience a different and deeper kind of fellowship with you.

And, Lord, if you can help me see beyond this pain to the purposes and meanings of it all, I will rejoice. Amen.

Integration and Integrity

One of the underlying themes of Job's story is integrity. God was impressed with Job's integrity. Job's wife exhorted him to curse God and die, trading his integrity for a momentary angry outburst. His "comforters" challenged his integrity, accusing him of some impropriety, since they all knew that sorrows like his came only to godless men.

And Job, himself, was committed to his own integrity: "Till I die, I will not deny my integrity" (Job 27:5). And he didn't. Although he did repent to God, acknowledging that he had declared things beyond his comprehension (see Job 42:3–6), Job never backed away from truthful and consistent faithfulness to his understanding of God's way in the world, even as that was modified by his experience.

Thanks to a recent rash of public failures of religious leaders, there has been a resurgence of interest in integrity. But it is interesting that the definition given in one book on the subject was as shallow as, "Integrity is doing what you said you would do."[6]

Integrity is *being* who you truly are.

No pretense.

No plastic.

No hype.

No hypocrisy.

Who you are is what you present to others, and people do what they say (which is faithfulness) because they *have* integrity. And they have integrity because they have been able to integrate around the only true center: Jesus, "the Christ, the son of the living God" (Matt. 16:16).

One thing that affliction does very efficiently is strip away the pretense. As Edward Kuhlman said, "When all the layers are peeled away, is there anyone home?" As we grapple with fragmenting personal pain, we learn who we are and what is the true quality of our faith.

That's okay if our faith is strong and unswerving. But very few of us fall into that category. In fact, very few people in the Bible, except Jesus, consistently fall into that category. For most of us, this grappling is like this letter from a pastor's wife, the mother of a child born with a defective heart:

> I am so tired of all the pressures—and yet incredible emptiness. All of the "answers" we give seem so phony. After spending almost sixteen years caring for a dying child—never a mother, just full time cardiac-nurse. The frustration is incredible. You suffered at the loss of a beloved child. I've lived in mourning since Marcy's birth—they said she would die. I could never love her. Somehow I go from total numbness to excruciating emotional pain. Trying to maintain a family—and a church—is quite a task. Somehow my faith has been bruised—and yes, shattered through the years.

My response: "Job's friends might say, 'You must be awful sinners!' Or your own friends may say, 'God must be meaning to use you powerfully. He's preparing you so!' And I would say, 'Life's really [abominable] sometimes!' You can take your pick. Actually, I think they're all true, but I think what we may resent most is when other people try to tell us WHY things have happened, instead of leaving this between us and God."

That's the bottom line: the truly important issues are between us and God. The way our responses spill over into the life of the kingdom is important to him too, but the key is that integrity allows me—requires me—to tell the truth. And that while I can truthfully say, "sometimes life's abominable," the difference faith makes is that I can also truthfully say I still believe God is on the throne.

In other words, while we hurt from the pain of it all, and we long for the freedom of the glory of the children of God, we can also see by faith where everything is heading. Our comfort and hope is knowing that he will one day make it right again.

Then why is so much lying encouraged or expected of you when you're struggling with long-term, unresolved pain? For one thing, people have elevated the heroes of faith and their dramatic stories of victory so much that they have unrealistic expectations of the rest of us.

For another, they have very little patience for our complaints. We make them so uncomfortable. Not only do they not know what to say, since they have already said all they know to say more than once, but in truth they don't want to be dragged down into our despondency and risk losing what little joy they may have themselves.

Finally, our continuing difficulty to resolve and rise to victory threatens them with the possibility that their little formulas and platitudes for living really don't work, or worse yet, that faith itself really doesn't make much difference.

But that's not what you would say, at all, if they could hear you. When you allowed Jesus to become the central integrating fact of your life, you happily discovered that pretense was no longer necessary. You can be who you are, and you can try to walk where he is leading. Yes, you are seeking to resolve things with his help, but as you do so, there will still be moments, perhaps even days, when you aren't "victorious," but struggling.

And what then?

Integrity.

Be true to yourself and most of all to God. Tell the truth. How does it really feel? He will never be surprised. Is every day with Jesus sweeter than the day before? Of course not. He had his bitter days too.

Maybe this whole week has been very hard, and playing their game is impossible. It's okay to refuse. Because the goal that grips you most is pleasing him, not them. And the hope that keeps you walking is the knowledge that he is on the throne and that he *will* make it right in the end.

That's where God is going in the universe. And that's where God is going with you, transforming your chaos into coherence through his presence in the center. He is freeing you to truthfully be yourself, maintaining a sense of integrity because you know that the most important thing is what he thinks of you.

He wants to help you communicate through your life a message of reality to a world of hurting people who long to know his hope in their despair, who are yearning for someone they can trust to help them understand the way to peace. Their needs are real, and it requires a real person with authentic faith to meet them where they are, inviting them to walk along.

Margery Williams creatively described the process of becoming real:

The Skin Horse had lived longer in the nursery than any of the others. He was so old that his brown coat was bald in patches and showed seams underneath, and most of the hairs of his tail had been pulled out to string bead necklaces. He was wise, for he had seen a long succession of mechanical toys arrive to boast and swagger, and by-and-by break their mainsprings and pass away, and he knew that they were only toys, and would never turn into anything else. For nursery magic is very strange and wonderful, and only those playthings that are old and wise and experienced like the Skin Horse understand all about it.

"What is REAL?" asked the Rabbit one day, when they were lying side by side near the nursery fender, before Nana came to tidy the room. "Does it mean having things that buzz inside you and a stickout handle?"

"Real isn't how you are made," said the Skin Horse. "It's a thing that happens to you. When a child loves you for a long, long time, not just to play with, but REALLY loves you, then you become Real."

"Does it hurt?" asked the Rabbit.

"Sometimes," said the Skin Horse, for he was always truthful. "When you are Real you don't mind being hurt."

"Does it happen all at once, like being wound up," he asked, "or bit by bit?"

"It doesn't happen all at once," said the Skin Horse. "You become. It takes a long time. That's why it doesn't often happen to people who break easily, or have sharp edges, or who have to be carefully kept. Generally, by the time you are Real, most of your hair has been loved off, and your eyes drop out and you get loose in the joints and very shabby. But these things don't matter at all, because once you are Real you can't be ugly, except to people who don't understand."

"I suppose you are Real?" said the Rabbit. And then he wished he had not said it, for he thought the Skin Horse might be sensitive. But the Skin Horse only smiled. "The boy's Uncle made me Real," he said. "That was a great many years ago; but once you are Real you can't become unreal again. It lasts for always."

The Rabbit sighed. He thought it would be a long time before this magic called Real happened to him. He longed to become Real, to know what it felt like; and yet the idea of growing shabby and losing his eyes and whiskers was rather sad. He wished that he could become it without these uncomfortable things happening to him.[7]

In relation to faith, "real" isn't magical, though it is supernatural. And it is uncomfortable, the result of merging the pain of living with the joy that knowing Christ can bring into a unique message that only you can give and that only he can energize.

11

Power from
the Pain

"AND WHERE DOES the power come from to run the race?" asks Eric Liddell, in the movie *Chariots of Fire*, as he delivers a sermon rather than run a race—even an Olympic heat—on Sunday. "It comes from within," he affirms, as the camera pans to a race being run, leaving us hanging, wishing for more from such a man of conviction. But evidently the modern secular mind from which the dialogue sprang could think of nothing more profoundly spiritual to say.

The problem with this answer is that it's only partly true, typical of many things that get us into trouble. It's also an exceedingly dangerous position for a person trying to move beyond fragmenting pain. "You've got to walk that lonesome valley," a song suggests, "You've got to walk it by yourself."

Noble, self-generated courage and resilience are the best we can muster by ourselves. Survival instincts take over in the struggle for composure, recovery, redirection. Hope lies in the "indomitable human spirit."

"Head high, chin out, steel your will, control your emotions, carry on, we'll just have to make the best of it." That's the world's way to deal with adversity.

The danger in this "wisdom" lies not so much in its possible failure as a coping strategy, as in its success without God. For any such success, admirable as it may appear by human standards, simply leaves us more at risk the next time, convinced of our own strength, sufficiency, and independence. The truth is this: egocentric grieving can never resolve the issues of pain, because suffering's primary lessons come from learning our dependence not our independence, our weakness not our strength, our helplessness not our sufficiency.

On the other hand, the power *does* come from within, deep within, from the very Spirit of God. His work is redemptive. Although he may choose not to intervene miraculously at our request—he could do even that—he is now here and his power to transform evil for good seems to be missed in Rabbi Kushner's famous conclusion:

> I believe in God . . . [but] I recognize his limitations. He is limited in what he can do by laws of nature and by the evolution of human nature and human moral freedom. I no longer hold God responsible for illnesses, accidents and natural disasters, because I realize that I gain little and lose so much when I blame God for those things. I can worship a God who hates suffering but cannot eliminate it, more easily than I can worship a God who chooses to make children suffer and die, for whatever exalted reason.[1]

I'd agree that God hates suffering, a result of the curse and part of the old order that he will someday eradicate. I might even agree that he cannot *yet* eliminate it globally. He is able, but hindered by his own sovereign timetable. To eliminate suffering would require obliterating the human race along with our realities, since both our realities and our personalities are permeated by sin.

But on a personal level, and sometimes even a broader scale, he does intervene directly to relieve suffering. God is still a God of miracles. And as to whether he *makes* "children suffer and die, for whatever exalted reason," my faith affirms that his purposes are always for our good. His heart breaks with ours when one of our children dies as a result of a natural catastrophe, an illness, or even a deliberate criminal act.[2]

God is not the author of evil and cannot be held responsible for the actions or consequences of evil people. Nor can the responsibility for genetic illnesses, disease, and death be laid at his feet, except in that he created man like himself, a free moral agent. But this was in itself a prescription for his own pain, even his own death. (Who can explain that?)

Yet that death was not fatalistic or forced. Although the necessity for the atonement was brought into being through Adam's choice, the Lamb of God still freely chose to become man. His decision to empty himself (see Phil. 2:6–8) was the divine reversal of the proclamations attributed to the evil one in his rebellion, "I will ascend. . . . I will make myself like the most high" (Isa. 14:13–14).

Certainly the suffering and death of our sons has immersed Kushner and me into paradoxes beyond our comprehension. But far deeper is the paradox of the suffering and death of God's own Son, Jesus. And this is why the suffering, death, and resurrection of Christ stand at the very apex of the history of man as well as of God's revelation of himself and his ways to man. These events are the key that unlocks the mysteries of suffering, giving us the hope and strength to carry on.

Now Satan is fond of reversals. He never tires of calling evil good and good evil, and his agents in our world energetically imitate their master. But the greatest reversal is God's. At the cross, Satan must have rejoiced, "Good. Now he is destroyed." Yet at that very moment, Jesus was dealing a death blow to the evil one (fulfilling the very first redemptive prophecy—see Gen. 3:15), setting men free from the fear of death (see Heb. 2:14–15), and giving them direct access to the throne of grace (see Matt. 27:51; Heb. 4:16). Soon after, he rose again to become an advocate with the Father for all those who would trust in him. Now at the Father's right hand, he intercedes for the saints (see Rom. 8:33–34).

In simple terms, the life, death, and resurrection of Jesus turned the realities of man upside down. And the same power that raised him from the dead became available through the Spirit for all who believe. As Peter Kreeft said, "Calvary is judo. The enemy's own power is used to defeat him."[3]

Satan is the enemy.

This is not a game.

It is war.

Our sometimes candy-coated Christianity inhibits our ability to perceive this truth, but in times of personal anguish we are able to see things as they are.

I'm not sure when I began to understand the events of these past ten years as spiritual warfare, but when Christopher was stricken, the issues began to clarify. Even more recently, as I've been considering a project with a colleague that would expose certain aspects of modern Satanic worship, I've been forced to consider the implications in terms of this warfare. Specifically, in pursuing this direction, I'm putting myself and my family at risk. A sobering thought when you consider the evil one's power in this world, and his past success in bringing us pain.

But as I thought and prayed, I claimed the blood of Christ—through which he broke the power of Satan and paid the penalty for my sin. If it weren't for Christ, I would have to contend with Satan on his terms and in my own strength. No contest. My sin would leave me powerless, since both he and I would know whatever evil might befall me, I deserved.

But Jesus placed himself—even physically, through his physical death—between the evil one and me, forever, despite my sin, because my sins were laid on him at the cross.

By faith, I placed myself and my family under God's mercy and protection. And I rededicated myself to the task he gave me. I know that nothing can happen to us in this continuing warfare except what will result in his glory if we are faithful.

Besides, if we who recognize Satan's presence (most of our culture does not) and who know of his method of operation (most do not) just walk away in fear, who will stand and fight? So, we put on the whole armor of God (see Ephesians 6), and we strive for the faith of the Gospel (see Phil. 1:27–30) with the power that God provides.

I recalled how even more recently, following a discussion with another physician, this time about the demonic in relation to freebased cocaine (crack), I verbalized my commitment something like this: "What more can happen to us? Can anything else occur that would be any worse than what has come to us already?" (I paused to ponder some rather gruesome possibilities in relation to that question, then continued.) "Regardless, I still will not bow down."

Spiritual Transcendence

Suffering can produce a certain transcendence or emotional detachment. "Do what you will, you cannot reach the real me." That was what Socrates had in mind when he affirmed that evil cannot harm a good man.[4]

It was also something learned by Viktor Frankl in a Nazi concentration camp and graphically described in his classic, *Man's Search for Meaning*:

I was struggling to find the reason for my sufferings, my slow dying. In a last violent protest against the hopelessness of imminent death, I sensed my spirit piercing through the enveloping gloom. I felt it transcend that helpless, meaningless world, and from somewhere I heard a victorious "Yes" in answer to my question of the existence of an ultimate purpose.[5]

This same quality of "spiritual transcendence" enabled some to express truly heroic generosity, even when the major issue for most was a simple matter of surviving. Again, from *Man's Search for Meaning*:

The experiences of camp life show that man does have a choice of action. There were enough examples, often of a heroic nature, which proved that apathy could be overcome, irritability suppressed. Man can preserve a vestige of spiritual freedom, of independence of mind, even in such terrible conditions of psychic and physical stress.

We who lived in concentration camps can remember the men who walked through the huts comforting others, giving away their last piece of bread. They may have been few in number, but they offer sufficient proof that everything can be taken from man but one thing: the last of the human freedoms—to choose one's attitude in any given set of circumstances, to choose one's way.[6]

Redirected Pain

Pain, any pain, can be redirected and creatively harnessed for God. As I grappled early on with Christopher's illness and possible handicap, the Lord brought a new friend, Bob McGlew, into my life. He was someone who had successfully helped his own daughter, Jenny, overcome a different rare, debilitating disease. She emerged from a long, difficult struggle with the belief that God has "blessed her" with what others would likely call a curse.

Jenny's disease (Ollier's disease) caused deformities in her hands and feet, and large tumors in the long bones of her arms and legs and also her hipbones, and it even involves her skull. She has had surgery on her hands and feet, and been hospitalized for pain control and biopsies. Bob and his wife, Margery, had struggled with Jenny's pain, as any parent would, but in it all they had tried to communicate to her a sense of her specialness to God. Just after her eighteenth birthday, Jenny sent them a note, which she has allowed me to include:

> Dear Mom & Dad, have a great weekend. I just wanted you to know how much I appreciate you both. I have been thinking a lot lately about my life and I've come to realize the truth of what you have been telling me about how God works since I was little. Pain was such an intrinsic part of my childhood, but looking back, I know that I would not be the person I am today without that catalyst. Living with my disease brought humility and introspection into my life. I now know that God has blessed me with this disease because he knew I would grow and learn from it. As you have said so often, he only places on us what we can bear, and I am thankful that he trusted me enough to bear and to benefit.

Creativity and Suffering

How many times have you said to yourself, "I ought to write a book about this"? How much poetry is there in your closet or desk, journaling your passage through the bitter and the sweet? For some reason, almost all the poetry I've written over the past twenty years or so has been composed in the context of losses. This one, written in 1987, reflected the situation after Christopher became ill:

I look into the Father's eyes
And wrestle with a thousand "Whys"
Why this? Why now? Why him, not I?
Why us, not them? I can't disguise
The hurt, the rage, unbridled pain
Erupting from my soul, again.
If that's the way it's going to be
Then build Your Kingdom without me.

But then, again, where can I go
To hear a word of hope, and know
The promise that beyond the pain
The ballad has a glad refrain
But what for now? And how can one
Still vocalize, "Thy will be done"?

And soon I hear a song begin,
Celestial, but from deep within.
A new, yet ancient melody
Of joy and pain, disharmony.
Or do the strains combine somehow,
A lovely paradox of sound?

Pain can be the energy that drives the poet, lyricist, novelist, painter, sculptor, creative artist. And creativity also brings pain, like the pain of childbirth. Consider this quotation of Søren Kierkegaard:

> What is a Poet? A poet is an unhappy being whose heart is torn by secret sufferings, but whose lips are so strangely formed that when the sighs and cries escape them, they sound like beautiful music. . . . And men crowd about the poet and say to him: "Sing for us soon again"; that is as much to say: "May new sufferings torment your soul, but may your lips be formed as before; the cries would only frighten us, but the music is delicious."[7]

Perhaps God has given you creative gifts, a talent that could be a blessing to others, and now you feel compelled to express the pain somehow. Do it! By all means, do it!

142

And don't let anyone discourage you. It may never be published, but then again it may. Perhaps no one will ever sing your songs, but then again, they may. And the paintings and crafts, the pottery and poetry, can be your gifts to God and others, statements of your inner journey, products of your pain, and at the very least some therapy for your own soul.

One of the earliest avenues of creative expression for Joni Eareckson Tada after becoming a quadriplegic was art, created by a flair pen held in her mouth! Now she sings, speaks, writes, and continues her artistry, traveling the world to tell how the Lord brings wholeness into human brokenness for his glory.

She has even established a special ministry to handicapped people, "Joni and Friends," another example of creativity through suffering. In your own world there are many who long for a word of hope, a healing touch, a smile, a song, a prayer. If you would give God your brokenness, asking him to use you creatively, it will simply amaze you how he'll do it. He knows where *you* are, and he knows where *they* are, so why should you wonder that he'll bring you together when the time is right?

A Word of Hope

For instance, Pastor Gerald Stigall was trying to minister to Mrs. J., a distraught mother in his Kansas congregation whose son was suffering with a serious asthmatic condition. Calling up a New Testament seminary professor, Dr. Grant Osborne, for pastoral guidance, he received a letter to Mrs. J. My thanks for their permission to use portions of it here.

I have had a fairly chronic asthmatic problem all my life. My first attack, I was told, came when I was eight days old. I had to spend at least two summers (while growing up) inside the house due to my condition. I am on fairly strong medicine to the present time. Further, I have been anointed with prayer on more than one occasion. . . .

In my case my asthma forced me into books and led to my academic career. *God knew better than I why he did not heal me.* I believe that we should learn to accept his "No" as a "Yes," that is, as a sign of his love because he cares enough to withhold what we think we want. . . .

It is not that God "doesn't want to heal [Jeremiah]" but that he knows better than we what is best for us. I can say that his refusal to heal me has "worked out for the good" (Rom. 8:28) in my life. May God comfort and guide you.

Power through Weakness

Dr. Osborne's perspective is similar to the apostle Paul's in 2 Corinthians 12:7–10 (quoted earlier). Strength from God comes through linking my weakness to his power by submitting to his sovereignty. His answer, which sometimes sounds like "No," can be heard as "Yes" if I listen with the ear of faith. In a sense, what sounded like "No," becomes a "Yes" when I say "Yes" to him.

Perhaps this is what the apostle had in mind when he spoke of *boasting* about weaknesses, or *delighting* in difficulties when the natural human tendency is to hide these things and to protect ourselves, whatever the cost.

If these assertions so contradict human wisdom, how can they be true?

First, this apparent paradox is true because the wisdom of God sometimes seems like foolishness to man (see 1 Cor. 1:18–25). In other words, a declaration like this may not immediately make sense to us. But that does not prove it is false. It may be that our normal categories, perspectives, values, and approaches are erroneous instead.

On another level, this paradox is another warning not to try to go it alone, in our own strength, because if we

144

do, we will most surely fail, *even* if we succeed. For if we "succeed," we'll be tempted to take the credit ourselves, which is failure in God's way of thinking. And then our focus might become our own power and faith, which seeks to glorify us rather than him.

In that case, we would have nothing of value to give others in need. Worse, we might be driven to afflict them with our formulas, disciplines, and principles of success—seeking to conform them to our own image. Instead, we should be pointing them to the real Source of strength in adversity, the Lord himself.

This leads to a third answer, if we stop for a moment and ask: What is God's greatest goal for us? What is his ultimate purpose in allowing us to experience the laboratory of pain? His one goal is that we become like the Master, proving to be his disciples, and so bring glory to the Father (see John 15). His purpose is that in becoming like the Savior, we become people who can touch other people with his healing power and grace.

Our personal research project in pain may be specially designed by him to help us learn we can overcome adversity *only* when we know we cannot overcome it by ourselves.

Is it possible that the *best* way for God to achieve his kingdom goals in us and through us is by allowing us to experience the pain it will take to learn these lessons of dependence? Further, do we reach the inevitable conclusion that his decision to discipline us (train us) in this way is a testimony to his love and grace?

The Sustaining Power of Grace

Or, to put it bluntly, does that mean suffering is good? For example, I've had lengthy discussions with several ministerial colleagues about whether it is right to call suffering evil. In one sense, I can understand their reluc-

145

tance to label anything that God allows "evil." After all, his intention is our good, our growth and maturity, our wholeness, and our contribution to his kingdom plan. And the result is good, if we're not casualties in the process. So are we forced to agree, in the end, "This experience of suffering was good"?

Some might take this to be Peter Kreeft's meaning, when, after quoting Saint Teresa, "Everything is grace," he says, "Suffering is something. Therefore suffering too is grace."[8]

But, "Murder is something, and rape, and child abuse, and satanic ritual, etc., but these are not good," I wrote to Kreeft. "Are they grace?" I continued, "Or is it that his grace provides the context in which any of these 'evil' things can be transformed (worked together) for good (a la Romans 8:28)? One of the implications of Romans 8:28 may be that God has to work at it because some things are not good, e.g., evil. Is there such a thing as evil?"

"Suffering is *made* good by grace. Not all things are good but grace makes them *work for* good," Kreeft explained in his reply. "God uses even evils, which he does not DO or WILL but ALLOWS because by his grace and our faith working together (he *won't* do it without us and we *can't* do it without him) he brings greater good out of evil." He adds, "But we do not *see* how he does it, nor do we see the end, heaven, which alone explains and justifies the earthly travail. So we never climb higher than Job. We do not become explainers, like the three friends; but we can without refutation be believers both in God's omnipotence . . . and love and the awfully real reality of evil. To let go of one of those three is fatal."

That fact that anything, even evil, can be redeemed by our loving God for his purposes and glory—the greatest goods—is a remarkable testimony to his power and his graciousness to involve himself to such a degree in the continuing struggle of our daily lives. However, when in his wisdom he allows us to experience what may be very trying times, *for our good*, we are still not forced to embrace the events as good in themselves.

Paul Tournier was videotaping an interview, when his own comment initiated a time of deep reflection on the significance of deprivation in his own life. (He was an orphan.)

> Being an orphan? I have always believed it to be the great misfortune of my life, and now I have to admit that it has been the great fortune of my life!
>
> A hundredth of a second later I imagined what a sick person would think if he heard me, a doctor, saying such a thing on the TV! I quickly corrected my aim, as you might say; I went on at once to say as I continued my stroll: "Obviously, I should never tell a patient that he was lucky to be ill." Fortunately, my reflexes were good—but the obvious contradiction left me in confusion. Was suffering not always evil? Could it be a blessing in disguise? Could evil be sometimes evil and sometimes good? It worried me: I had to know! . . .
>
> [The fact that creativity awakes in times of suffering is not discussed much] because for too long we have made the mistake of looking on suffering as a good thing. In the Middle Ages especially it was a favorite theme. . . .
>
> The fact is that evil is everywhere mixed with good. The Bible proclaims the fact and our experience confirms it. . . . There is a mixture, but no confusion. Good is the cause of good, and evil causes evil. Evil cannot be the cause of good.
>
> What then of the relationship that exists between deprivation and suffering, and creativity—apparently between evil and good? But relationship is not the same as cause.[9]

Because a painful experience is the occasion for growth does not mean the event itself is good, Tournier might say. And he concluded that events themselves are morally neutral. Evil and good, he explained, are in people, not events.

In other words, meanings are connected with intentions. So it becomes easier to label Auschwitz, or child abuse, or rape, or everything done with evil intentions as evil. But what about asthma, Ollier's disease, leukemia, or genetic disorders? In my mind, they are evil too since their root is in the curse, and the curse came about because our first parents fell into sin through Satan's evil intentions and his cunning deceit.

I refuse to call the illnesses that brought death to Jonathan and disability to Christopher anything other than evil. It is true that the suffering these experiences has brought to us has been—and continues to be—redeemed for good by God, but even that is more a statement about him and his power than it is an affirmation that there was anything good in the events themselves.

Conclusions
and New Directions

12

To Kiss the Joy

Celebrating What Is

I HATE TO tell you this, now that we've walked this far, but the final lesson—doctoral level at the University, Pain 601—is this:

- It never really ends.

At least it never ends in the way we wish it would, and the way others wish it would. For instance, I've been asked, and have even posed the question myself, "How do you know when it's over?" Sometimes I think I'm getting close to an answer, such as:

- When I'm able to think of the person (or the loss) with joy instead of a nagging feeling of anguish.
- When my mind is no longer controlled by remorse, anger, or a need for revenge.

- When I can ask questions other than those unanswerable ones that begin with "why."
- When my day is not filled with statements that begin with "if only."

In one sense, it *can't* be over. The experience is now an integral—and I hope integrated—part of who I am. No one can perform the surgery I long for, taking away the pain, along with its cause, never to be heard from again.

Yet surgery is a good analogy. Recovery may take weeks, during which there is a diminishing sense of pain. Finally the incision is healed and some normalcy restored. I can get on with living—permanently scarred, and occasionally reminded of my personal adversity by a look in the mirror.

Early on as you walk with pain, there may be many reminders. News stories will flash on your television screen:

- Plane crashes, terrorists suspected.
- Flash flood traps school bus, eighteen feared dead.

Or you'll notice headlines in the newspaper:

- High school student killed by drunk driver.
- Teacher accused of child molesting.
- Two-year-old dies in backyard swimming pool.

Or it may be that your neighbor's dog is hit by a truck.

Pain is all around us, all the time. But personal losses sharpen our awareness of the suffering in our world. The injustice, insensitivity, and misery may rise up without warning and drag you back into the pit.

The intensity of your reaction may surprise you. Suddenly, when you thought it was *over*, you're thrust back

152

into the feelings again—rekindling a level of anger, even rage, that you had not thought possible. Or maybe you react, instead, with a sense of futility, even cynicism, or its flipside, sarcasm.

Even positive things can trigger the pain. You'll be at a restaurant and remember her. Or his class will graduate, and you'd like to feel the joy of all the other parents, but all you can think about is "If only he hadn't gone out that night."

Either way, without warning, some event beyond your control will tap your own buried emotions, and like the tapped sugar maple in March, you *will* bleed.

I thought that when I got to the end of this book, I would finally have it worked out, be able to put the subject down, and walk away, somehow turning my attention to more positive themes. God's way, after all, leads toward joy.

But the closer I got, and the more I thought about it, I realized that to tack a happily-ever-after ending on an otherwise truthful story would be uncharacteristic and unhelpful. If I did, you might then feel driven to try for an obligatory resolution yourself—rainbows or sunsets and Prince Charming kissing Sleeping Beauty awake—when for you the fairy tale settled into nightmare quite some time ago.

The song we're singing has two themes:

- Humanly speaking, life is painful.
- Spiritually speaking, life is joyful.

How can both be true?

Early in his missionary days, Dr. Paul Brand would travel by ship to and from India. During the voyages, the renowned physician would often join the crew at dawn and dusk as they sought to fix the ship's position by using the sextant, a two-scoped navigational instrument.

One scope was fixed on the horizon, and the other on a known star. By using charts and trigonometry, they could get their bearings even on the open sea.

Sometimes the experience of loss leaves us bobbing like a rowboat on the open sea, without a clear sense of where we are, where we're headed, or which way home is.

Often, the standard evangelical message to such mariners, is "Fix your eyes on the Lord," ignoring the sometimes painful horizons of human reality (suffering, alienation, etc.). Most hurting Christians are too weak to resist. Or they submit to the single scope approach through training or fear. The partial result is that while they may get a fix on God, they still can't really figure out *where* they are in the process of grieving, or more importantly, in the process of living.

On the other hand, skeptics fix their single scope on the horizon—human realities, even positive human endeavors—in an effort to overcome the pain, but in reality they never rise above resignation (called by Kubler-Ross, "acceptance"[1]) and ultimate despair.

Some "religious navigators"—Rabbi Kushner included—may utilize a second scope, trying to get a fix on divine as well as human realities. But they fail because that "divine" star is not where they demand it to be—God's ways do not conform to their requirements or expectations. These poor sufferers never truly know where they are, either, even when they think they've got their bearings.

The only helpful approach uses both scopes: the horizon of experience—as when I agree that, humanly speaking, "Life can be excruciatingly painful"—*and* the divine, which beckons, "Trust Me, anyway, and I'll redeem even this evil for good in the end."

So, let's change the question. Instead of asking, "How can I know when it's over?" let's ask, "Where am I in the process that leads beyond the pain, even to joy?"

154

Expectations

When I spoke to one psychiatrist friend about my intention to call this last chapter, "Celebrating What Is," he reminded me that when you're in despair, celebrating may be impossible. The process of recovering, he added later, is like finding islands in the sea, and as things get better the islands are closer together. But it's not all solid land. In between, you step into the water again, over your head, and wonder if this time you might drown.

When you're in despair, *survival* is a more realistic goal than celebration. But gradually, with the help of God, your family, friends, and possibly even a professional counselor, you begin to sort things out, fixing both scopes on realities again, and you begin to hope. Here is my best advice.

Give yourself time. Some things cannot be rushed. No instant masterpieces here. God's workmanship (see Eph. 2:8—the Greek word is *poiema*, from which we get the word *poem*) is you! You and I are God's creation. We might even say we are his "poetry," his way of singing a song of hope to a broken world.

Give yourself space. Don't let anyone force you into his mold. Your relationship with God is the main issue. What does he think of you? What does he ask of you? People may offer their own interpretations and perspectives on these questions. But the final issues are between you and him. And he is more kind, loving, gracious, gentle, forgiving, and creative than any of us can imagine.

Give yourself truth. Don't play anybody's game, even your own. No pretending allowed. No hypocrisy required. You can be yourself. If you force it, it will just take longer. If you fake it now, you may never be able to tell when it's real.

155

Progress

Sometimes we're such perfectionists. We miss the fact that we're progressing, because all we can see is that the goal of becoming like Christ seems to stay so distant. "But I'm so far away," you lament. "Sometimes it seems I'm making no progress at all."

No one will ever be perfectly like Christ, this side of glory. But, as someone has suggested, the key question at any point in time is this: which way are you facing—toward him or away from him? Or, more specifically, which way are you moving—toward him or away from him? If you asked God for ways to measure your progress, you would hear words like "becoming," "increasing," and "developing."

Becoming is a process word. Are you becoming a person of faith?

Increasing is a dynamic word. Do you have an increasing sense of hope, linked to him and his promises?

Developing is a maturation word. Have you been developing a loving concern for the needs of others—so many of them—who are hurting too?

Faith is God-directed. You may not see yourself as a pillar of faith. But are you still walking—even if sometimes you're just stumbling along? That's faith. We walk by faith and not by sight. If we walked by sight, we would have jumped off a bridge a long time ago. And haven't you discovered, because of—not in spite of—this journey, that trusting is the only way to any real peace of mind? We only *thought* our lives were in our own control. Experience has shown us that is a lie. The fact is, we never had the control in the first place.

What about hope? Hope is future directed. It is a confident expectation that God will keep his word, that he is going somewhere, in the universe and in your life, and that he will make it turn out right in the end.

And love? Love is giving, and it is other-directed. Christ loved me enough to consider my helpless needs more important than grasping his equality with God, so he laid his rights aside, took the form of a bond-servant, becoming obedient even to the point of his atoning death on the cross (see Phil. 2:5–11).

By contrast, grief can be so self-directed. For days, weeks, months, or even years, the focus is what *I* have lost, what *I* have endured, what *I* have suffered. Part of this is self-pity, and partly it may be self-protection. For didn't loving give birth to my pain, allowing me to make such an emotional investment in the subject of my sorrow? Perhaps it was a hope or a dream, a goal or a thing desired such as good health, success, or prosperity. Most likely it was a person, and loving that person that much is what left me at risk. As C. S. Lewis said,

> To love at all is to be vulnerable. Love anything and your heart will certainly be wrung and possibly be broken. . . . The only place outside heaven where you can be perfectly safe from all the dangers and perturbations of love is hell. . . . We shall draw nearer to God, not by trying to avoid the sufferings inherent in all loves, but by accepting them and offering them to him . . . throwing away all defensive armour. If our hearts need to be broken and if he chooses this as the way in which they should break, so be it.[2]

One way to know you are moving beyond the pain is when you begin to be *willing* to risk loving again, knowing far better than before the potentialities inherent in that choice. This is truly progress, a key marker on the trail that leads toward joy. Not long after Jonathan's death, I expressed the difficulty of this choice:

Dilemma

My boy, the joy had just begun,
But suddenly your life is done

157

And, stunned, I, lonely, wander on
Without you, an automaton.

I wonder, dare I love again,
Or was our loving all in vain,
A passing pleasure tinged with pain?
Am I to live or just remain?

Tormented by the nagging fear
That one, once loved, will disappear,
Should I withdraw or venture near?
Is there an answer that is clear?

"Withdraw! Withhold!" my heart replies.
"To love again would be unwise!"
Yet something whispers otherwise,
That only loving satisfies,
Beautifies, or edifies.

Experiencing What Is

As long as my focus is primarily on the loss, my emotions are so heavily invested in the past that I may be oblivious to the life, love, and joy continuing around me. For instance, many bereaved parents become so obsessed with their loss that they lose sight of each other's present needs, as well as the needs of surviving siblings. So what was devastating in itself has a magnified effect that is not easily overcome. The sad result is a ripple effect of deprivation with long-term and far-reaching implications for the entire family system.

Can you free yourself to experience life in the now? It's not disloyal to laugh again, to enjoy the little things like the garden, wildflowers, birds, or a good meal with good friends who care about you *today*.

Can you take pleasure in the friends and family you still have, entering into their todays and even their plans for tomorrow? Simple as this suggestion may sound, it remains one of the most difficult hindrances on the road

158

to wholeness. I recall how—more than six years after Jonathan's death—a dream, coupled with the guidance of a gifted counselor in a group setting, helped me realize I needed to forgive the past and embrace the present. In my dream, a large bird crashed and burned. This was the death of my hopes and dreams for Jonathan. Out of the ashes arose a butterfly—his new life.

As we discussed the dream, I began to "see" Jonathan's face, and I thought about what he might say to me, things like: "I love you. I'm sorry you hurt so much. Don't be afraid to love Christopher, Allison, and Dana. Be free. Be happy again." I knew he would want me to let him be who he really was now. I realized that the face I would see when I thought of him wasn't really him. He had changed. And one of the most significant lessons came in the message, "Forgive Mommy." For all those years I had held her responsible for his death, and now I knew I had to forgive her—and *be forgiven* myself—to get on with living.

If Jesus were here, he would deliver a similar message.

But Jesus is here. He is the Lord of *now*. When God revealed his true name to Moses, he called himself: "I am" (Exod. 3:14). He, the self-existent one, dwells somehow in an eternal present tense, beyond what we call time, yet involved in its every moment.

One of the more remarkable claims of Jesus was that he was the same "I am" (John 8:58), a claim so enormous the Jewish listeners immediately sought to execute him for blasphemy. But if Jesus *is* the great "I am" (which explains how he can be "the same yesterday and today and forever" [Heb. 13:8]), then he was not only *here* on earth two thousand years ago. He was here at creation too (see John 1:1–5). He will be present at the future renewal as well. But the most significant thing in terms of my personal emergence from the mountains of pain is that in every present moment of every painful day, he is here and he is Lord.

This means Jesus was here (and he was Lord) when the event occurred that brought my sorrow. He felt it with me then, and he feels it with me now. He will share that pain with me every moment of every day that I continue to carry it until (and even after) I wisely decide to cast it upon him (see 1 Peter 5:7).

When I finally invite Jesus into the now of my pain, emptiness, and loneliness (or, more realistically, every time I "finally" do that), I hear him gently inviting me into the now of his present peace and joy.

The peace Jesus gives has a transcendent quality, like his ability to transcend as well as enter into our realities. It "transcends all understanding, [and] will guard your hearts and your minds in Christ Jesus" (Phil. 4:7).

The joy Jesus gives is also transcendent, allowing us to rise above the painful realities of life while at the *same* time truly experiencing the pain. The apostle Paul is navigating with both scopes as he succinctly describes his journey of faith: "Dying, and yet we live on; beaten, and yet not killed; sorrowful, yet always rejoicing; poor, yet making many rich; having nothing, and yet possessing everything" (2 Cor. 6:9–10).

"Don't worry. Be happy!" is not *God's* message to the brokenhearted soul. Although the pursuit of happiness is supposed to be a U.S. citizen's inalienable right, the inevitable losses of life easily demonstrate its superficiality.

While many well-meaning comforters (along with some critics) have exhorted you toward happiness and away from your pain, a more realistic, biblical goal is "sorrowful, yet always rejoicing." The apostle had endured many hardships and trials. His many sorrows had a variety of sources—like his wayward spiritual children in Corinth, or perhaps his regret over having persecuted the early Church, and even earlier being an accessory in the murder of Stephen. His sorrows were real, sorrows like yours and mine, yet because he never lost his fix on God and his purposes, he could always rejoice by faith regardless of the circumstances.

In the same way, we are able to rejoice (even if this joy is mostly an inner, sustaining reality for now) and to give thanks.

> Be joyful always; pray continually; give thanks in all circumstances, for this is God's will for you in Christ Jesus.
>
> 1 Thessalonians 5:16–18

How I feel about the circumstances *is* important, but just as important, if I'm going to move beyond the pain, is my sense of humble gratitude to God for what he *has given*, what he *has done*, and also what he *is doing*.

By contrast, my horizon-oriented scope searches for what is lost, at least in the beginning, and I am hurt, perhaps indignant when I cannot find it. "What have I done to deserve this?" I ask, sometimes humbly, sometimes as if God owes me an explanation. With healing of soul—my mind and will as well as my heart—I begin to see more clearly through both scopes, becoming thankful for his generosity in the past, his sustaining grace in my pain, as well as his commitment to transform that pain into ministry for his glory.

This changing perspective is another way to know you are emerging into the light again. It may take awhile, but you will find that in your continuing search for answers, some of the questions themselves will change. This was a necessity for those who struggled to survive the Nazi concentration camps. As Viktor Frankl explains,

> What was really needed was a fundamental change in our attitude toward life. We had to learn ourselves and, furthermore, we had to teach the despairing men, that *it did not really matter what we expected from life, but*

rather what life expected from us. We needed to stop asking about the meaning of life, and instead to think of ourselves as those who were being questioned by life—daily and hourly. Our answer must consist, not in talk and meditation, but in right action and in right conduct. Life ultimately means taking the responsibility to find the right answers to its problems and to fulfill the tasks which it constantly sets for each individual.[3]

As Christians, we know that "life's" name is *Jesus,* who said, "I am the way and the truth and the life. No one comes to the Father except through me" (John 14:6).

We know that our source of life has pointed us to right answers to our problems in his Word. He has also laid hold of us for a purpose: "I press on to take hold of that for which Christ Jesus took hold of me" (Phil. 3:12). And he has set before us certain tasks to fulfill as his disciples, among them:

Remain in me, and I will remain in you. No branch can bear fruit by itself; it must remain in the vine. Neither can you bear fruit unless you remain in me.

I am the vine; you are the branches. If a man remains in me and I in him, he will bear much fruit; apart from me you can do nothing. . . . This is to my Father's glory, that you bear much fruit, showing yourselves to be my disciples.

John 15:4–5, 8

Therefore go and make disciples of all nations, baptizing them in the name of the Father and of the Son and of the Holy Spirit, and teaching them to obey everything I have commanded you. And surely I will be with you always, to the very end of the age.

Matthew 28:18–20

While we may not know the reasons why God has allowed specific events to take place in our lives, in the

Scriptures we can clearly discern his overarching purpose:

> We know that in all things God works for the good of those who love him, who have been called according to his purpose. For those God foreknew he also predestined to be conformed to the likeness of his Son, that he might be the firstborn among many brothers.
>
> Romans 8:28–29

God's purpose for us is that we become like his Son—our brother—whatever it takes. And what if learning to be like him requires suffering? It should be no surprise. Jesus himself learned through suffering:

> Although he was a son, he learned obedience from what he suffered and, once made perfect, he became the source of eternal salvation for all who obey him.
>
> Hebrews 5:8–9

We begin to understand the sufferings of Christ—to know him more personally, and what it meant for him to hurt—as we share in those sufferings today (see Phil. 3:10) through our own pain and through hurting with others. Somehow, in the process, we are doing our part, as Paul said,

> I fill up in my flesh what is still lacking in regard to Christ's afflictions, for the sake of his body, which is the church.
>
> Colossians 1:24

The reason I'm still here (and not with the Father already) has something to do with learning obedience and becoming more like Christ. Beyond that, though, I'm still here to carry on the work of Jesus, who pointed people to the Father in their struggle for meaning, purpose, fulfillment, and joy within this riddle—life. Since there is nothing lacking in Christ's afflictions in relation to his redemptive work at the cross, there must be another meaning, if I am to add anything to his afflictions, for the sake of his Body, the Church.

What is missing—now—is Jesus's personal, tangible, physical presence. What he lacks is a substitute, a representative and spokesperson to say for him, "I know that life is sometimes terribly difficult, but God is still on the throne, still working all things for the good of those who love him. So, keep the faith, and look beyond the pain where there is hope, and peace, and joy."

This is the purpose for which Christ has laid hold of me. The sometimes intense pain has been the pain of birthpangs—not my own, as if I could give birth to my own destiny, but God's with me, as he has walked with me, and sometimes carried me, through this darkness and back into the light again.

My purpose is to know God, to please him, to be found faithful to him, and even to be known as his friend. And I have tried to be your friend too, speaking the truth in love (see Eph. 4:15), perhaps even wounding you in the process (see Prov. 27:6).

I have given you myself. It is the least I could do, as well as the most I could do. But it is not really so remarkable as when you consider that Jesus would do the same, as he has done and continues to do even now.

Of all the questions that linger, the most urgent by far is his: What will you do with him, with his offer of himself as Savior and Lord, yes, even of your broken life? And what of his purpose and calling, and the task—or is it, rather, a privilege—of sharing in his continuing sufferings in this world, transforming the pain into power for his kingdom? Will you accept, or even embrace, *your part* in filling up what is presently lacking in his afflictions by reaching out in love to others in pain, with a reality-oriented, compassionate message of healing and hope that springs from the very heart of God?

Just for a moment, project yourself to the end of your own life. Looking back to this very moment, what would you need to see between now and then to think of your life as fruitful for God and faithful to his calling?

If you can answer that question, perhaps you're ready to move ahead, for there is no time better than the present to echo the apostle's words: "Forgetting what is behind and straining toward what is ahead, I press on toward the goal to win the prize for which God has called me heavenward in Christ Jesus" (Phil. 3:13–14).

But if you are honestly not ready to move ahead just yet, your Lord understands. Though he longs to heal your broken life, he is patient and kind and willing to listen to your continuing lament until you can truthfully say, "Enough."

And someday, looking back, he'll help you see how he can use even your present pit of despair as a foundation for a dwelling place more lovely than you could dare to ask or think.

In the meantime, friend, I invite you to start over, at the beginning, when you're ready, and perhaps in time we'll pass this way again.

Afterword

CHRISTOPHER IS DOING well, thank God. This morning the kids were playing outside in our pool, carrying on like most kids—boisterous, exuberant, happy. An uninformed listener might think they haven't a care in the world.

They do, of course, as do we; though we tend to ponder the negative possibilities more than they—conscious that our genetic "sword of Damocles"[1] hangs over us all even as we try to enjoy the feast of life.

For a couple of years Christopher saw discernible progress after the illness that left him with brain damage. We watched him go through the development stages again: crawl, walk, even run. I'll never forget being at his school and seeing a banner, "Congratulations! Chris Biebel ran a half mile 5/4/88!" And he hadn't even told us.

He has done well in school too, keeping up with his class, even excelling in some things, like the spelling bee he won in the spring of 1989.

The recovery has leveled off now, leaving him with some deficits to overcome—physically, emotionally, developmentally, and in other areas. We are getting help, and glad it's available—because the frustrations with our present limitations versus what *is* for others or what *might have been* for us sometimes hinder our ability to live joyfully in the now as we walk into a future only God knows.

In describing this continuing pilgrimage, I've chosen to use collective words, because living with disability really is a problem that impacts us all. While Chris continues to grapple with a wide variety of personal issues, the rest of us in this family system sometimes struggle too. In the process there are many opportunities for growth toward maturity, but there is also the persistent temptation to run away or dull the pain through inappropriate means.

This is the burden borne daily by people involved with long-term unresolved situations such as extended illness or disability, even divorce. How better could we learn that some things are even harder to live with than death, even the death of a child?

We have learned many other things too—like how hard it is to face your contribution to the continuing problems when you thought that survival itself had been a rather remarkable achievement.

Or, just recently, I began understanding how a pending joy can actually cause anxiety if you've been sad so long you're almost addicted to it.

I wanted this book to be for people in pain, not just for bereaved parents, or parents with handicapped children. And this is why I chose not to tell our story to the exclusion of yours. While ours has been a particularly difficult journey, pain is pain, and pain is all around.

In one sense, this book still isn't finished, for life is a special university and as we keep living we keep learning. So until God is finished with us here, the last chapter *can't* be written.

Then again, maybe the last chapter will be written by someone else, like Allison, or Dana, or a son who makes his father proud, Christopher Lee Biebel.

The end . . . to be continued.

Notes

Chapter 1: Educated at the University

1. Edward Kuhlman, *An Overwhelming Interference* (Old Tappan, N.J.: Fleming H. Revell Company, 1986), 18.
2. Peter Kreeft, *Making Sense Out of Suffering* (Ann Arbor, MI: Servant Books, 1986), 15.

Chapter 2: Crisis

1. Kuhlman, *An Overwhelming Interference*, 24–25.
2. Peter Kreeft, *Love Is Stronger Than Death* (San Francisco: Harper & Row Publishers, 1979), 115.

Chapter 3: Confusion

1. Kreeft, *Making Sense Out of Suffering*, 57.

Chapter 5: Putting the Pieces Back Together

1. Kuhlman, *An Overwhelming Interference*, 45.

Chapter 6: God Loves Me

1. William Shakespeare, *Macbeth*, Act V, Scene v, lines 23–28.
2. From the newsletter of Carney Evangelical Free Church of Carney, Michigan. Used by permission.

Chapter 7: Suffering Has Value

1. Kreeft, *Making Sense Out of Suffering*, 169–70.

2. *Time*, October 26, 1987.

3. Kreeft, *Making Sense Out of Suffering*, 101.

4. Ibid., 137–38.

5. Used by permission.

6. A. W. Tozer, "True Faith Must Influence Our Daily Living," *Renewed Day by Day*, G. B. Smith ed. (Harrisburg, PA: Christian Publications, 1980), June 7.

7. Some of these thoughts were inspired by Bill Gasset's song, "Too Wise to Make a Mistake," copyright 1984, Image VII Records, Inc.

Chapter 8: Jesus Wants Me Whole

1. Used by permission.

Chapter 9: Loving God in a New Way

1. C. S. Lewis, *The Four Loves* (London and Glasgow: Collins Fontana Books, 1970), 112.

2. Lewis Smedes, *Choices: Making Right Decisions In a Complex World* (New York: Harper & Row, 1986), 23.

3. James Stewart, *The Strong Name* (Grand Rapids: Baker, n.d.), 126–27.

4. Ibid., 145.

5. Elizabeth Barret Browning, "Sonnets from the Portuguese," *A Concise Treasury of Great Poems*, ed. Louis Untermeyer (New York: Pocket Books, 1966), 284–85.

6. Laurie Klein © 1978, 1980. House of Mercy Music, Maranatha Music. Used by permission.

Chapter 10: Toward Integration

1. Used by permission.

2. "The Second Coming" reprinted with permission of Macmillan Publishing Company, from *The Poems of W. B. Yeats: A New Edition*, ed. Richard J. Finneren. © 1924 by Macmillan, renewed 1952 by Bertha Georgie Yeats.

3. Augustine, *Confessions*, 1.1.

4. Francis A. Schaeffer, *True Spirituality* (Wheaton: Tyndale, 1979), 142.

5. See Schaeffer, pages 18–45, for more on this subject.

6. Ted W. Engstrom and Robert C. Larson, *Integrity* (Waco: Word, 1987), 10.

7. Excerpt from Margery Williams, *The Velveteen Rabbit* (New York: Avon Books, 1975), 16–20. Reprinted by permission of Doubleday, a division of Bantam, Doubleday, Dell Publishing Group, Inc.

Chapter 11: Power from the Pain

1. Harold S. Kushner, *When Bad Things Happen to Good People* (New York: Schocken Books/Avon Books, 1983), 134.

2. For a more complete discussion of the problem of evil and a refutation of Kushner's conclusion, see Kreeft, *Making Sense Out of Suffering*, especially 36–37.

3. Ibid., 132.
4. Ibid., 60–63.
5. Viktor Frankl, *Man's Search for Meaning* (New York: Beacon Press/Washington Square Press, 1985), 60.
6. Ibid., 86.
7. Kierkegaard, quoted by Kreeft, *Man's Search for Meaning*, 75.
8. Kreeft, *Man's Search for Meaning*, 143.
9. Paul Tournier, *Creative Suffering* (San Francisco: Harper & Row, 1982), 22, 25, 27–28.

Chapter 12: To Kiss the Joy

1. Elizabeth Kubler-Ross was a pioneer in the field of death and dying. She is well-known for her book *Living With Death and Dying* (New York: Macmillan, 1982), which outlined five stages of grieving.
2. Lewis, *The Four Loves*, 111–12.
3. Frankl, *Man's Search for Meaning*, 98.

Afterword

1. "In Greek legend, a courtier who overpraised the happiness of the tyrant Dionysius the Elder . . . was forced to sit at a banquet under a sword suspended by a single hair that he might learn the perilous nature of that happiness." *The Reader's Digest Great Encyclopedia Dictionary*. Copyright © 1966, 1968, 1971, 1975 The Reader's Digest Association, Inc. Pleasantville, NY, 338.

David B. Biebel is a writer and health educator. Presently he is editor of *Today's Christian Doctor* (Christian Medical & Dental Associations [CMDA]; Bristol, Tenn.—since 1992) and president of Hope Central Ministries. He's the author of many articles and several books besides this one, including *Jonathan, You Left Too Soon* and *How to Help a Heartbroken Friend*. He often writes and speaks in workshops and in seminary and conference settings on the theme of "Joy Again"—from loss to recovery/renewal. He lives in Conifer, Colorado.